Everyday Spirituality

Prof. Badrinarayan Shankar Pawar received his PhD from Oklahoma State University in 1996 with the highest possible cumulative grade point average of 4 out of 4 for the PhD study components. He has about two and a half decades of teaching and research experience while serving in distinguished academic institutes, including the City University of Hong Kong, the Indian Institute of Management Ahmedabad, the Indian Institute of Management Kozhikode, the Indian Institute of Management Indore, XLRI—Xavier School of Management, Jamshedpur, and the National Institute of Bank Management, Pune. He is currently a professor at the Indian Institute of Management Raipur. For about the past 16 years, his research has focused mainly on workplace spirituality, primarily been published in international journals, and been extensively cited.

Everyday Spirituality

Lessons from the **Ordinary Life** of a
MOTHER

BADRINARAYAN
SHANKAR PAWAR

Published by
Rupa Publications India Pvt. Ltd 2024
7/16, Ansari Road, Daryaganj
New Delhi 110002

Sales centres:
Bengaluru Chennai
Hyderabad Jaipur Kathmandu
Kolkata Mumbai Prayagraj

Copyright © Badrinarayan Shankar Pawar 2024

The views and opinions expressed in this book are the
author's own and the facts are as reported by him which
have been verified to the extent possible, and the publishers
are not in any way liable for the same.

All rights reserved.
No part of this publication may be reproduced, transmitted,
or stored in a retrieval system, in any form or by any means,
electronic, mechanical, photocopying, recording or otherwise,
without the prior permission of the publisher.

P-ISBN: 978-93-6156-165-8
E-ISBN: 978-93-6156-691-2

First impression 2024

10 9 8 7 6 5 4 3 2 1

The moral right of the author has been asserted.

Printed in India

This book is sold subject to the condition that it shall not,
by way of trade or otherwise, be lent, resold, hired out, or otherwise
circulated, without the publisher's prior consent, in any form of
binding or cover other than that in which it is published.

I dedicate this book to my late father, Mr Shankar Hari Pawar, and my late mother, Mrs Chandrabhaga Shankar Pawar, for the amazingly lofty standards of spirituality, morality, idealism, purposiveness, dedication, courage, diligence and altruism they practised and through which they provided to me many ideals to pursue. This book is dedicated to them with gratitude for their countless contributions to my life and for their blessings. While dedicating this book to them, I pray that they and God forgive me for any shortfall in my service to them.

Contents

Foreword ix

Introduction xi

Part I
BAAI'S STORY

1. A Short Childhood and an Early Marriage 3
2. The Middle Phase of Baai's Life 18
3. The Later Phase of Baai's Life 27
4. The Old-Age Phase of Baai's Life 42
5. Baai's Declining Health and Her Journey towards Her Eternal Abode 55

Part II
BAAI'S LIFE: A LESSON IN SPIRITUAL STRENGTH

6. Baai: An Embodiment of Noble Virtues 75
7. Facing Hardships by Oneself, While Serving Others 85
8. Baai's Approach to the Adversities of Life 92

Part III
DRAWING TOGETHER THE SPIRITUAL ELEMENTS IN BAAI'S LIFE

9. A View Based on the Scientific Literature on Spirituality	103
10. A View Based on the Scriptures	121
11. Reflections on Practical Spirituality	150
Notes	165
Acknowledgements	180
References	182

Foreword

Dr Badrinarayan Pawar (or Badri, as he is affectionately known by me and others) is the most virtuous, honest, compassionate and humble person I have ever met. I was his dissertation advisor at Oklahoma State University; I have known him for over 30 years and it is my great honour to pen this foreword.

Having read about his mother's life, I now have a much better understanding of Badri and what shaped his philosophy of life. He is truly his mother's son, as his approach to his life very much mirrors his mother's spiritual journey. The values he mentions—acceptance, contentment, positive life purpose, industriousness, determination, kindness and compassion, forgiveness, and ethicality—have always been guiding principles in his life.

During his doctoral studies, Badri's work ethic was 'legendary'. So much so that I began to become concerned about his health. Badri would work on his research for three or four days in a row, without stopping for rest or nourishment. He lost so much weight that I convinced him to see a doctor. He was told that he needed to consume more calories, as he was malnourished. It was difficult for Badri to eat the additional food, as he felt that he was being wasteful and that others might need this food more than he did. Like his mother, he felt obliged to sacrifice his own well-being for the sake of others.

I share my perspectives on Badri with you so that you will know that the ideas shared in this book are presented by someone who has lived by these principles. Badri has thought deeply about spiritual issues his entire adult life, and his research acumen has enabled him to read and study extensively on spirituality writings. Although I was his 'teacher', it was Badri who taught me a great deal about how one should live one's life, for which I owe him a great deal of gratitude. You will find this book to be enlightening, regardless of your religious background and experience.

—Ken Eastman, PhD,
Dean Emeritus,
Spears School of Business,
Oklahoma State University

Introduction

This book describes various aspects of the inspirational life of my late mother, who used to respectfully be called 'Baai'. Reading about her life will give readers a deep insight into a life steeped in spirituality. She exemplifies how spiritual development can unfold without separating oneself from life's ups and downs, and without being a follower of any sect or spiritual master.

This book is divided into three parts. Part I of the book focuses on Baai's life story, from her childhood till her leaving for her heavenly abode, and offers deep insights into the foundational principles of her life. Part II then helps one understand the overarching spiritual principles that show up in various areas of her life. Finally, in Part III we look at the spiritual elements in Baai's life through the view of the scriptures and also of the scientific literature on spirituality.

While spiritual development may be difficult for readers to comprehend, the duties, dilemmas, challenges and adversities in one's life are real. In this context, Baai's life is a guiding path that illuminates the readers. She not only exhibited *karma yoga* (union with God through work) and *bhakti yoga* (union with God through devotion) during her lifetime, but also exhibited the horizontal and vertical dimensions of transcendence as dimensions of spirituality. The horizontal dimension of transcendence reflects how one functions in relation to other people, communities and creatures, while the vertical dimension reflects how one maintains a connection with the sacred or the divine. Spirituality is not a separate realm but an integrated way of living one's ordinary life. Baai's life is a poignant example of the same; it elucidates the spiritual teachings in scientific literature and in the holy scriptures.

∽

On 17 December 2017, in the intensive care unit (ICU) of a hospital, Baai left her physical body for her heavenly abode. Even during her penultimate moments of physical discomfort, she experienced serenity and peace. The profound experience of peace during her final moments resembles the descriptions of liberation and self-realization that have been etched out in the scriptures. Though she had lived an ordinary life, she was at the same time extraordinary.

She was around 90 when she passed away, and had been in and out of hospitals for about two months. She had undergone two surgeries on her brain in a month. A plastic drain tube was attached to her head to drain the fluid from her brain, and bandages covered the surgery wound on her scalp.

For quite a few weeks, she had a feeding tube inserted through her nose, accompanied by an oxygen mask to aid her weakened breathing. Immobility and other health problems had caused her body to swell. Her hands were secured to bedside bars to prevent her from dislodging the oxygen mask and other tubes. She was also heavily medicated. In the end, her body was riddled with medical support equipment, including a nasal feeding tube, a surgical wound fluid-draining tube, an oxygen mask, a urinary catheter, a diaper, pressure strips, and bandages on her arms and legs. She could not have a meal or drink water naturally through her mouth for some time.

However, even in that frail, aged, vulnerable and medically-assisted state, Baai's face was astonishingly clear. Her memory was sharp; her mind was fixed on God. She was the epitome of compassion. On that day, I, her youngest son, visited her at the ICU around noon. Baai was uninterruptedly chanting God's name, '*Raam, Raam, Raam, Raam...*' As I placed my palm on her forearm, she stopped chanting, looked at me and said, 'Your body is cold.' When I told her I had come from outside and brought my lunch with me, she asked, 'Who cooked for you, and what curry was prepared for you?'

After gently massaging her legs, I asked her how it felt. She replied, 'It feels very nice.' Then I asked her if I could kiss her cheek, and she responded in the affirmative. After kissing her cheek or forehead, I asked how it felt. She replied, 'Very sweet.' She said to me, 'Please study well.' In this final interaction, minutes before she passed away, there was no trace of regret, grief, lamentation or anxiety. Instead, there was a sense of peace.

I exited the ICU and prayed while seated in the hospital's waiting lobby. In a few minutes, the ICU staff announced that her heart had stopped beating. It was then that I realized that Baai was in the state of being liberated.[1]

A few weeks before that, during my conversation with her, I had asked when she would return home from the hospital. She had calmly replied, 'We will return home whenever there is the God-wished moment to do so.' She had further added, 'We will go wherever God takes us.' The attendant nurse said that whenever Baai was awake at night, she would chant God's name. This suggested that she was in a state of union with God (*yoga-sthiti*).[2]

I had been reading the sacred text *Dnyaneshwari* in the waiting area outside the ICU. It explains that a person who knows that the physical body is perishable and that the true nature of oneself is unbounded, and who, at the time of leaving the physical body, is aware of all-pervading God, unites with the divine. It further explains that whatever one has craved throughout life is what one's mind remembers at the time of leaving one's body, and this impacts the form one takes in the next birth. Therefore, one must ceaselessly remember God throughout one's life.[3]

Dnyaneshwari adds that one should do one's deeds in the service of God, and devote one's mind and intellect to the Almighty. By doing so, one becomes united with God—one is liberated, or, in other words, mentally disengaged from the physical body and identifies oneself with the imperishable Supreme Self.[4] *Dnyaneshwari* mentions that when one does the constant practice of connecting one's mind with God, the mind becomes one with the divine consciousness and remains unaffected by the concerns of leaving the physical body.[5]

This description of a liberated person, and my observations of Baai at the time of her leaving her physical body, made me reflect on how she lived: on the surface, an ordinary life while facing several adversities, and yet she could attain a state of union with God and was finally liberated from the 'concerns' of leaving the physical body. This also led me to reflect on how Baai could maintain the lifelong and ceaseless practise (*abhyaas yoga*), or the process of connecting her mind with God and doing all her actions in the service of God.

> ### GLEANINGS
>
> Baai experienced serenity and peace in her final moments despite extreme physical discomfort. Her profound experience of peace reflects the descriptions of liberation in the scriptures. Her lifelong practices, and the scriptures, show us that one can attain union with God-consciousness by:
>
> - lifelong and ceaseless practice of connecting one's mind and senses with God
> - performing all actions in the service of God
> - practising bhakti yoga or devotion to God

PART I
BAAI'S STORY

1

A Short Childhood and an Early Marriage

Baai was born to a poor family in a small village, possibly named Nanegaon or Malegaon. Her exact date of birth is unknown because birth certificates were not readily available then. It is estimated that she was born between 1925 and 1930. This chapter mainly encompasses the period of her life from childhood to adulthood.

Baai's family members did not have any education, regular employment, a secure source of income, land, property, or even their own house. Her family did not even have any resourceful relatives or acquaintances that could provide support. Her father, a casual farm labourer, was the primary earning member of her family. Her mother was a casual labourer and performed other jobs as well. Baai was one of four children (two brothers and two sisters).

When Baai was a young girl, her father had an accident while drawing water from a well using an ancient water-drawing device (*mot*), in which a large, water-filled leather bag is drawn out of a well with a rope tied to a bullock. This accident rendered him immobile. In those days, medical treatment was not readily available in rural areas. He was the only earning male member of the family, and the family greatly depended on his earnings for its subsistence. In such circumstances, his immobility caused considerable hardship to the family.

He would have suffered both physical pain, due to his leg injury, and mental trauma, due to his immobility and loss of income. Baai's mother too would have suffered considerable emotional anguish: crestfallen because of the accident, not being able to provide medical treatment to her husband, and the hardships of maintaining her family's livelihood. Baai's father passed away soon after the accident. Possibly, the fractured leg may have led to medical complications, leading to his untimely death (at the age of about 45). This was a tremendous blow to Baai's family.

Baai's mother, whom the children addressed as Lahaani Aai (younger mother), now had the onerous responsibility of feeding the family. Lahaani Aai now moved to another village. Someone compassionately provided her with a vacant house, next to an animal shed, to live in. Even before sunrise, she would work on a *chakki* (stone equipment used to mill grains). Operating this equipment entails continuously gripping the wooden handle of the heavy stone disc on the top and rotating it by turning the handle. The food grain between the two stone discs is crushed into fine flour as the top stone disc rotates upon the lower one.

Using the chakki to make flour for other families, Lahaani Aai received some money, food grains, and sometimes food items such as buttermilk. This work was completed during the early part of the day. For the rest of the day, Lahaani Aai cleaned temples in the village, made garlands for deities, filled oil in the lantern in some faraway temple and, in return, received money, food grains, and other food items from the temple owners. She also did other work, such as casual farm labour. Baai assisted her mother in various jobs, including her grain-milling work before dawn. The family's poverty did not allow Baai to have decently stitched clothes. As a child, she would simply wrap some leftover piece from an old torn-out sari around her waist and tie her hair with a cord.

Baai's elder brother would sell food grains in a distant town to buy vegetables for his vegetable-vending work in the village. From the food grains Baai and Lahaani Aai earned from their labour, a portion would be allocated for the family's consumption, while the remainder would be set aside to be taken to the distant town by Baai's elder brother. There, he would purchase vegetables for his vegetable-vending business. This was laborious work, as he had to carry heavy food grains in a creel on his head to the town, and then carry a creel filled with vegetables on his way back.

Baai's younger brother also did petty work, such as working as a peon in a school or as a night-duty security guard at a warehouse. However, because of his spendthrift nature, it is unlikely that he contributed much to the family's livelihood. Thus, most of the family's financial burden fell on Baai and Lahaani Aai. Due to a lack of access to any guidance or education, the family remained impoverished. When they performed farm work as casual labourers, they sometimes did not receive money but were paid in kind (for example, they received green lentils to eat).

The monsoon season was tough, as very little farm work would be available. Baai would also involve herself, as a casual labourer, in making large-sized clay bricks used in house construction. This was back-breaking work, as it involved digging soil, carrying large soil-filled baskets on the head, carrying water from the river in large containers, and mixing the soil and water to prepare a thick clay slurry, which is cast into bricks by pouring it into moulds. After an exhausting day at work, Baai would sleep peacefully by the side of Lahaani Aai.

Neither Lahaani Aai nor Baai had any long-term ambitions like buying a house, moving to another town, or buying agricultural land or even fancy clothes for themselves. They lived life day to day, working and subsisting on whatever they received from laborious work. Even during such hardship, they both upheld certain principles such as honesty in doing their work, working efficiently, and doing their work by regarding it as their God-ordained duty.

Baai would go to temples at night to listen to scriptures being read. She would observe a fast on *Ekadashi* (an auspicious day occurring every fortnight). While grinding grain during the wee hours of the morning, she would immerse herself in the work while singing devotional songs (*abhanga*) that glorified God. Thus, her work transformed into a service of and devotion to God.

Lahaani Aai was a stickler about cleanliness. Even the old, torn clothes that she used to wear would be kept clean. Knowing that the responsibility for providing shelter, livelihood and happiness to her children was on her, she would try to muster tasty meals for them on festival days. She had to be creative in cooking special meals within her limited means. For example, by adding jaggery to water and boiling the mix, she would prepare a sweet liquid (*goolavani*), which was then eaten with a roti made with sweet-paste stuffing. Also, a curry (*aamati*) would be made using water drained from boiled split gram.

Thus, even in poverty, Lahaani Aai discharged her responsibility of providing festive meals to her family members by carefully thinking and planning, applying her skill and labour, and remaining frugal given the material constraints. Baai would certainly have imbibed these virtues after watching her mother's hard work, creativity and perseverance. Despite her occasional disruptive behaviour, Lahaani Aai exhibited extraordinary calm and would not even reprimand her sons. In such instances, she would suffer quietly in anguish and shed a tear. Suffering silently, rather than scolding and shouting at her children, showed her compassion and mercy.

As was the custom in those days, Baai was married at an early age, around 12. Soon after the marriage, she went to stay with her in-laws in another village quite some distance away. Baai's in-laws were also a poor family with no land, but they did have a house of their own. Baai's father-in-law was a tailor.

Her in-laws were harsh towards her and made her do strenuous work. Her work would begin a few hours before sunrise, with going to the crematorium on the outskirts of the village to collect cow dung for fuel. As few people visited the crematorium, it provided a quiet place where stray cattle could loiter without being disturbed by people. The cow dung was required to make dried cow dung cakes that were used as fuel for the *chullah* (a clay-made primitive stove), and to prepare its slurry to be applied as a thin coating to settle the dust from the soil floor of the house. As a child of 12, it must have been scary for Baai to visit the crematorium just before daybreak. However, her sense of obedience, fear of punishment, and helplessness left her with no choice.

Baai was aware that she came from a poor family, had lost her father, and did not have a responsible brother. Thus, she bore all the work given to her. She did not want to burden her widowed mother with her woes, and bore those stoically. As the villagers slept, she walked the narrow and rough village lanes, full of small ditches and protruding stones on the surface. There were only a few lamp posts with wick lamps for illumination at a few selected places. The cremation place used to be engulfed in darkness. No doubt Baai would have stumbled, faltered and even sustained bruises on her toes. She would shiver in the winters and get drenched in the monsoons. Her mother was miles away and had no means of communicating. To whom could she turn to talk about her sufferings? She undoubtedly prayed to God for strength to endure the hardships and grief.

After collecting cow dung from the crematorium, Baai would do grain-milling work to prepare adequate flour for the family. Using the hand mill in her in-laws' house, she would also do grain-milling work for other relatively affluent families in exchange for buttermilk or money. The milling had to be done in the dim light of a wick lamp. The work was strenuous, as one had to apply manual force to rotate the large stone wheel constantly. Once, she was so exhausted that she fell asleep while working on the grain-milling equipment. She woke up abruptly after being slapped by her mother-in-law. The rest of the day would pass by while doing various other household activities, followed by paid work as a farm labourer on a distant agriculture farm. Each day was exhausting and full of drudgery, with no affection from her in-laws and no one to share her feelings with.

The freedom, choice and affection that she had been used to at her mother's house were now replaced with restrictions, helplessness, intimidation and harshness. She was also usually provided leftover food. Not even milk from the household cow was provided to Baai. Even the special and simple delicious items that she prepared for the family on festive occasions were not shared with her.

Lahaani Aai had taught Baai to be polite, submissive, tolerant and uncomplaining. She had advised Baai that, when faced with hardships or ill-treatment, she must suffer and endure rather than resist or retaliate. Thus, Baai quietly endured all these hardships at her in-laws' with a sense of duty, acceptance, forgiveness and compliance.

Occasionally, Baai used to be sent to her mother's home for a few days. Her father-in-law, or her brother from her village, would accompany her on an arduous journey that took about two days on foot. Since lodges were unavailable, they would sleep for one night in a shelter provided by any merciful villager. However, if no one provided any, they would halt at a spot close to a well or river to drink water. Then they would eat rotis with groundnut chutney and sleep under a tree. When Baai was still a child, she could not keep up with the adults. She would trail behind her father-in-law, who would stop, turn around, see how far behind she was, and then continue. By the time she arrived at the village, she would be fatigued but happy to be meeting her family.

Apart from all the work she was involved in at her in-laws', she also had to fetch water for the entire family from a distant well. This work was done either in the morning or late at night. It involved strenuous activities like drawing bucketful water from the well by pulling the bucket with the aid of a rope tied to it, emptying the water from the bucket into a large pitcher, then lowering the empty bucket into the well and repeating the process till the large pitcher was full. She would carry the pitcher on her head and walk the long distance towards her house. At the house, the water from the pitcher would be emptied into a large storage drum. Often, Baai simultaneously carried three water-filled pitchers by placing two pitchers (one on top of another) on her head while perching the other above the waist and supporting it with her arm. This work required multiple trips from the well to home every day.

Following water-fetching, she would prepare breakfast and meals for the family. Finally, she would leave for her daily labourer's job in a distant farm field. Due to this, Baai would usually be late in reaching the farm and to cover the time lost, she would work hard at a rapid pace. This too involved arduous labour. Holding weed strands in her hand, she would loosen the soil around the weed root with the sharp point of the front edge of the sickle, and then uproot the weed and place it in a heap.

She and other labourers were at the mercy of the vagaries of nature. Sometimes it would rain and they would get drenched. They would try to protect themselves by using old jute sacks, making a cap-like slot at one end by folding it and then placing that cap-like part on one's head, while the remaining jute sack covered the shoulder and back. However, if there was a heavy monsoon shower, even this jute sack would offer little protection.

Baai would carry her packed lunch to the field. The meal would contain a few pieces of *bhaakari* (bread made with the food grain *jawar*), with some dry curry or chutney wrapped in an old, tattered cloth. The meal bundle would be kept under the shade of a tree until the lunch break. Baai and her co-labourers would fetch drinkable water from a nearby well or stream. She would often miss breakfast while completing several chores at home. Yet, even when she was having her lunch hungrily, she would share a part of her meagre meal if she saw that any co-worker had inadequate food or no food at all. Her generous, altruistic and compassionate self expressed itself even when she had a paucity of food.

On her return home, there would be more household chores waiting for her. After completing all the day's activities, she would have to get up just after midnight to start her morning tasks of going to the crematorium to collect cow dung, followed by the strenuous work of grain-milling. And so the toil and drudgery continued.

Yet, despite the workload, undernourishment, lack of affection and care from the in-laws, and harsh treatment, Baai did not avoid any work given to her. Even in such an adverse situation, Baai practised the virtues of acceptance, contentment, industriousness, doing one's duty, honesty, forgiveness, service and compassion. Her being was filled with altruism, compassion and devotion to all those around her. She viewed all her work as God-ordained duties. Baai felt happy when her husband and in-laws were happy with her work, and when the distress of people around her was alleviated by her deeds.

Her harsh life—full of emotional, physical and social hardships—did not get any easier when she was expecting a child. On one occasion, during the advanced stage of pregnancy, her legs were swollen, as she had spent the entire day standing and uprooting jawar crop plants. This work also caused blisters on her palms. Even after the delivery of her child, she did not have access to nourishing food. Within days, she resumed her strenuous daily routine of heavy work. She carried her baby to the field where she toiled as a casual labourer, with the baby tied to her body with a large sheet of cloth made from an old sari. At times, while working in the field, Baai would place the baby on a cloth under a tree and then carry on cropping grass or clearing the field of weeds. One day, the baby woke up, crawled a short distance, and got entangled in a dried, thorny plant and experienced great pain. Baai felt torn by not being able to sit with her baby even for a few moments, as there was too much work to complete.

Baai had a sense of sincere duty towards her husband and her in-laws, and worked hard to fulfil her duties towards her family, often at the cost of her own nourishment and rest. Often, she was so exhausted that she could not fall asleep. While facing so many difficulties, Baai used to always remember God and chant God's name. In her old age, she told one of her sons that the right way to balance spiritual and worldly activities was to softly murmur or chant God's holy name while doing one's work. To explain this, she used to recite from an abhanga, *Kaama madhye kaam, tumhi mhana Raam*,[1] meaning 'to chant God's name (Raam in this case) while doing one's work'.

Baai had a deep urge for religious and spiritual advancement. During *kirtan*s (devotional singing along with spiritual discourse), she would wrap up her strenuous work of the day and sit in the evening kirtan till late at night, listening intently to the devotional singing. Later, she would reflect on this, internalize it, and narrate or discuss the teachings with others.

In the village temple, some portions of religious scriptures were read by a wise person at a gathering of devotees every evening. It would take a few months for the entire scripture to be read. Baai would regularly go to the temple for those sessions and intently listen to, reflect on and internalize the guidance from the scriptures. At times, she would go for the readings skipping dinner. And she would listen intently till late at night, sacrificing the short window she had for sleep. So intense and genuine was her devotion to God.

As part of her religious activities, Baai would also visit holy places of pilgrimage, such as Paithan, Alandi and Pandharpur. Each of these places of pilgrimage has a distinct spiritual significance. Paithan is the place where Sant Shri Eknath Ji Maharaj lived. Alandi is the place where Sant Shri Dnyaneshwar Ji Maharaj was born and is also the place where he took *samadhi*.

Taking samadhi is an act of withdrawing from the world where the body gradually ceases to function and one's consciousness gradually separates from the physical body and merges into the divine consciousness.

Pandharpur is the place where Sant Shri Pundalik Ji Maharaj lived and where, as per the faith of devotees, Lord Pandurang descended to bless Sant Shri Pundalik Ji because of his dutiful service to his old parents.

Even during those pilgrimages, Baai's compassion and altruism would shine forth. Before setting off for the pilgrimages, she would arrange for food and other necessities for those family members who would remain at home. Because of poverty, Baai would carry food and cooking ingredients such as jawar, *besan* (split gram flour), chilli powder, salt and cooking oil. At the location of the pilgrimage, she would reside in a free shelter provided by a charitable organization. She would bathe in a nearby river, wash her clothes, and thereafter proceed to places of religious activity. She would spend most of the day attending *pravachan*s (religious discourses) and kirtans.

At that shelter, she would create a temporary chullah by adjacently placing two to three large stones to create a closed space for the fire to be lit. Wood for fuel and cooking utensils would be provided by the shelter owner. With this arrangement, she would cook simple meals in a short period. For her children, she would carry some delicacies like laddus and other sweet items made out of flour, jaggery and oil, which could last a few days without getting stale. Upon returning home from such pilgrimages, Baai would begin clearing up the backlog of work piled up at home due to her absence.

While serving her in-laws, husband, children, relatives and guests, she maintained an active involvement in religious life by going to temples to listen to scriptures, attending spiritual discourses, and going on pilgrimages. Often, she would practise *japa* (silent repetition of God's holy name) during her work. While Baai lived in impoverished circumstances, she wished to create a bright future for her family, particularly her children. Thus, Baai ensured that each of her children went to school.

In those days, village parents often did not send their children to school but engaged them in petty money-earning roles to supplement the family's daily earnings. Not so for

Baai; she would make extra effort to get her children ready for school while also ensuring they had neat and clean clothes. To pay more attention to her children's education, she left the farm labourer's job and took up work in the kitchen of the school's hostel, which was located a few minutes' walk away from her house. This required her to cook for some hours in the morning and some hours in the evening, and allowed Baai to pay attention to her children during the day.

Baai's commitment to providing her children with good education as a pathway to a bright future imposed further hardships on her. In due course, her eldest son had to go to a distant town to attend college, as college education was unavailable in her village. This required money for room rent, food and other daily requirements. To supplement her earnings, she did several other jobs besides cooking in the hostel kitchen. For example, she began cooking and serving meals to a teacher who came from another town. She also took part in cattle-rearing and would earn money from selling the milk of the cow (affectionately named Fulaambri) and the she-goats that the family owned. Keeping the cattle and their stable clean, getting fodder for them, milking them, and delivering milk to the households considerably added to her packed schedule.

Baai's husband, whom the children and others used to address as 'Bhaau', was a tailor. He rented a shop in the village for his work. His work used to be seasonal, as villagers would usually put in an order for new clothes only during the annual festival of Deepavali or during the wedding season. At such peak times, the volume of tailoring work suddenly increased and he had to work day and night. To avoid feeling sleepy, he sometimes skipped dinner and took some extra tea to keep himself alert.

To further supplement the family's livelihood, Baai also began to toil hard on the farms, taken for cultivating from the farm owners by her husband. In this arrangement, Baai and Bhaau were the tillers who would take care of all activities, from sowing to getting the food grains a few months later. This involved ploughing, sowing seeds, removing weeds, and protecting the crop from flocks of birds.

Once the crop plants were ready, these would be made into sheaves of manageable sizes. The sheaves would be tied together by some cord-like weed to make them tight. Large piles of sheaves would then be moved in a bullock cart from the field to the village, where the crop ears (*kanees*) would be cut from the rest of the crop plant. The sheaves would then be stacked orderly to be used as fodder for cattle for most of the following year. This stacking was a laborious process.

The entire process would take a few months, from the initial field preparation to obtaining grains. For this work, Baai used to receive some of the cultivated grains as payment. Some of the grains would be used by the family and extra grains would be sold. A few years after marriage, the hard work for Baai and her husband paid off, as they managed to buy a small piece of agricultural land to cultivate.

GLEANINGS

Baai imbibed several of Lahaani Aai's virtues: industriousness, honesty, cleanliness, a sense of duty, absence of anger, forgiveness, mercy, devotion to God, a sense of acceptance, and being happy in life. Baai's lifelong practices show us that one can attain union with God-consciousness by:

- accepting one's life circumstances and life obligations, especially those events that are beyond our control (for example, one's physical characteristics, intelligence, the kind of parents one is born to, etc.). This reduces negative emotions such as grief, frustration and sadness, and paves the way for positive work for self and others. Ultimately, this sense of acceptance is conducive to spiritual development in the form of bhakti yoga.
- being compassionate and generous, even to those who are harsh to you and also in the face of scarcity of essential resources such as food.
- being industrious and honest, having a sense of duty, and believing that this can be fulfilled as a service to God.
- connecting with God in many ways such as japa while doing one's work, and listening to scriptures and spiritual discourses. These reflect elements of bhakti yoga and karma yoga as mentioned in the scriptures.

2
The Middle Phase of Baai's Life

The middle phase of Baai's life spanned from about 20 to about 45–50 years (up until 1975). This phase was marked by insurmountable challenges. Her husband, Bhaau, became ill due to some problem with his abdomen. Before this, as mentioned previously, his tailoring work used to peak during festive seasons and the wedding season in the summer. Everyone used to get new clothes stitched for the festival of Deepavali. These peak seasons would require Bhaau to fulfil several tailoring orders, which meant working long hours day and night. The heavy workload, at times skipping meals, and working for long periods without rest likely led to his subsequent health problems. Bhaau had to undergo abdominal surgery, following which he used to feel tired and his feet would swell after only a few hours of work.

Thus, after surgery, his tailoring work gradually came to a halt. He had been a skilful tailor known for his excellent work, and he also had a high level of sensitivity and self-respect. Being unable to provide for his family made him irritable over a period, and this in turn made Baai sad. She now had to manage the livelihood of eight members of the family. At this time, Baai's father-in-law was ill as well; her eldest son was studying in a distant town, incurring heavy expenses; and Baai's only daughter had attained marriageable age, necessitating the need to find funds.

In the period following Bhaau's abdominal surgery, the family faced a tragedy. His only sister, Keshar, was not treated well by her in-laws. One day, Baai's family received the news that Keshar was severely ill. Bhaau travelled with a friend in a bullock cart to meet her. As he had undergone abdominal surgery only a few days ago, he had to tie a cloth around his abdomen to protect himself from the severe jolts caused by the rough village roads. When he reached the village, he found his sister had head injuries and high fever, and was in a semi-conscious state. Bhaau and his friend tried to provide her with medical treatment. However, it was too late and she passed away. It seemed that she had been beaten up by her in-laws. Furthermore, she did not receive any medical treatment for those injuries and hence developed a fever and became critically ill. By the time Bhaau reached her village, the damage was done.

As Baai's in-laws lost their only daughter in such a ghastly episode, the entire family was devastated. For months, Baai's father-in-law, out of grief and despair, spent most of his time in a local temple and would come home only for meals. All were grief-stricken at this loss. Bhaau's health deteriorated, possibly because of the difficult and jolty bullock-cart journey when he was still in the process of recovery, and also because of his grief over the shocking death of his sister.

During this period, Baai's virtues of acceptance and forgiveness were strikingly displayed. After some time, a relative from another village visited Baai's home. He had been instrumental in arranging the marriage of Baai's sister-in-law. While it was natural for her to feel negative emotions towards him, as an expression of her duty towards a guest visiting the home, she did not express any anger but treated him with customary hospitality.

In this middle period of her life, around 1970, there was a drastic shortfall of rain in her village and surrounding areas for a few consecutive years. This led to drought and famine, and food shortages in several villages, further devastating several families. As farming had mostly stopped due to the drought, agricultural work was not available for anyone, and thus even this form of livelihood ended for Baai. As the tailoring work had come to a halt due to Bhaau's ill health, the family had to vacate the rented tailoring workroom, and sell the sewing machine and the large wooden table used to mark cloth measurements. Parting with these items was a painful experience for Baai's family.

Due to the severe drought, there was no green grass for the animals to graze on, and a lack of crops also made fodder unavailable. Some cattle-rearing families had no choice but to abandon their animals in open fields to fend for themselves. Baai's family had a few she-goats and one cow. The cow was greatly attached to Baai because Baai would tenderly clean, caress and feed her. The cow used to bellow when she would see Baai approaching the cowshed. Baai had to make the painful decision of selling off the cow, as fodder or grass were unavailable, thus jeopardizing the cow's survival. The market for trading animals used to operate once a week in a distant town. For a benign person like her, it would have been an excruciatingly painful experience to walk towards the animal market to sell off the cow that she had reared with great love and care. She must have felt immense sadness while returning to her village after selling the cow.

Similarly, she had to sell off the she-goats too. The only solace she would have received while selling off the cow and she-goats was that she was giving them an opportunity to receive food and water from their new owners. She viewed such compelling circumstances and traumatic incidents as part of God's design, and managed to get through such difficult phases by doing japa.

∽

Yet another blow to her family came around that period when their small piece of agricultural land was taken away by the government, as it went under the water-release zone for a new dam being constructed at a distant place named Jaaikwaadi. The amount received as compensation for the land was primarily used for the marriage-related expenses of Baai's daughter. Around the same period, her father-in-law became severely ill, and his medical treatment put an additional burden on the shrinking income of the family. She rendered every possible nursing care and service to him, such as removing mucus from his nose and occasionally even from his throat, and emptying the bedpan whenever full. With the absence of modern sanitation facilities in villages those days, rendering such nursing service to an old, bedridden person required performing tasks that many may find repulsive. However, Baai expressed her compassion and sense of duty.

To save some money, they supplied their eldest son (who was studying in a distant town, as mentioned previously) meals cooked at home so he would not have to buy food elsewhere. However, this was a laborious task, as the college was about 70 km from her village. The roads in those days were of poor quality and the government-owned buses were the only mode of transport for long-distance travel. One such bus used to leave her village around 7.00 a.m., and reach the distant town around 11.00 a.m. She would wake up early in the morning and prepare good meals consisting of a relishing curry and several pieces of bhaakari. The food would be packed in a sizeable, round-shaped tin food container, and then be taken to and placed on the bus for the onward journey to the town.

During this period of struggle, as a programme to sustain the livelihoods of people during the severe famine, a government agency started digging a quarry outside Baai's village. This provided a source of employment to the village people. The work was to break off large stone pieces from the base and walls of a large pit (dug deeper to make a quarry out of it) through explosives-induced blasts. The large stone pieces were then required to be broken manually into small-sized pieces using hammer blows. Thus, this work produced small stone pieces for projects such as road construction and also created a quarry as a potential water source for the village. As the explosions loosened and shattered stones from the quarry walls and base, some small stone pieces would fly off in the air and posed the risk of injuring the labourers. Baai had no choice but to perform this risky and laborious work, and that too under the harsh heat.

After school hours or on school holidays, Baai's children also joined in this work. Once, I hurt my finger and the wound festered for quite a few days. This must have caused considerable anguish to Baai. On another occasion, her hammer blow fell on her finger instead of the stone, causing an injury. It used to pain so much that on some nights she could not even sleep. Nevertheless, she had to continue her strenuous hammering work and the hectic daily chores because of her duty to feed a large family.

As the drought had caused considerable food shortage in the village, those working in the quarry received a food powder named *sookadi* through a government agency. Sookadi contained one or more flours roasted with a bit of oil, to be consumed as a substitute for regular food items. However, the smell and taste were such that one could consume only a bit. Baai and her family members had to consume this powder cooked like porridge on some occasions, and sometimes even have it raw. Another red-coloured inferior food grain *millow* was also made available through the government ration outlets. On some days, Baai and her family had to eat bhaakari made out of it.

∽

She went through several painful episodes but faced them all with endurance, acceptance and equanimity. Once, she visited the matrimonial house of her daughter, who lived in a large city about 200 km away. As she was the only person in the family who could do the household work, Baai prepared some non-perishable food items as meals for her family members before leaving. She would have felt considerable anxiety about visiting her daughter because, in those days, the matrimonial house of a married daughter had considerable social and relational dominance over the daughter's parents.

As direct buses were unavailable, she had to change buses and reached the city after a journey of about 10 to 12 hours. Baai alighted from the bus at the bus station and walked from there. As her family had been facing the dismal circumstances of a severe drought and fell into extreme poverty, she had to walk barefooted from the bus station. Upon reaching her daughter's prosperous matrimonial house, she discovered that her daughter was being harshly treated by her mother-in-law, including finding faults in trivial matters and depriving her of adequate and timely meals. She had married off her daughter in this prosperous family, bearing huge expenses beyond her poor family's capacity, hoping that her daughter would get a better life. Seeing her daughter's suffering caused her immense grief. However, she endured these painful experiences, knowing that her daughter had at least escaped poverty. Such was her sense of acceptance and equanimity that she said it was as if she was placing a stone on her chest while she swallowed her tears.

Over time, Baai's eldest son graduated, got married, and moved to the distant city of Pune to live with his wife. To provide money for his shifting to Pune, she had to sell her *mangalsutra* (a sacred ornament signifying the married status of a woman). Shortly, some money was required for his job-searching process, and for this they had no choice but to borrow from a moneylender after mortgaging the house.

In this phase of her life, Baai had to go through several ordeals such as a severe drought, loss of agricultural land, loss of house's ownership, loss of cattle, husband's ill health, loss of husband's capacity to do productive work and earn, selling off her mangalsutra, and selling off the sewing machine and tailoring table. Also, as mentioned previously, in this period, Baai's daughter was married off. To meet the marriage expenses, the family had to spend most of the compensation amount received from the dam-related government agency that had taken over their agricultural land. A year after the marriage of Baai's daughter in 1971, her old and ailing father-in-law passed away, and about three years after his demise her mother-in-law passed away too.

Such numerous adversities and dismal circumstances marked the middle phase of Baai's life till she attained the age of about 45–50 in 1975. She continued to view the adverse circumstances as God-ordained, and her actions as God-ordained duties. Even in this dismal situation and amidst a demanding routine, Baai would thank God at the end of the day for having seen her through the day's responsibilities. She would reaffirm her faith in God to help her discharge her responsibilities the next day. Thus, her devotion to and faith in God did not waver but became stronger.

GLEANINGS

- While facing several adversities, Baai demonstrated a sense of acceptance and equanimity. Equanimity, or evenness of mind, is union with God (yoga)[1].
- Baai maintained a mind free from anger. Keeping oneself devoid of agitation in adverse happenings is among the

qualities that characterize a person with a steady mind and intellect (*sthitpradnya*).[2]
- Baai practised compassion and forgiveness. These two are among the qualities that make a devotee dear to God.[3]
- Baai's approach to life had a self-sacrificing and other-serving orientation, along with a sense of duty. In discharging her duties, she did not avoid work just because it was arduous (such as breaking stones in the harsh summer heat), or because it was repulsive (such as nursing her old and ailing father-in-law with almost non-existent modern sanitation facilities). Avoiding one's God-ordained duties out of attachment (*moha*) is a form of ignorance (*tamas tyaga*)[4] and avoiding God-ordained duties to escape the distress or inconvenience to the body is a mode of passion (*rajas tyaga*)[5]. Rather, discharging one's God-ordained work out of a sense of duty and without a sense of attachment or desire for the fruits of work is renunciation in the mode of goodness (*saatvik tyaga*)[6]. Such renunciation facilitates liberation[7] and self-realization or self-knowledge[8].
- In summary, instead of shirking responsibilities due to laziness or involvement in wrongdoing (traits associated with tamas) or avoiding discomfort and seeking pleasure (traits linked with rajas), true renunciation is to practise such activities as God-ordained work out of a sense of duty, without seeking personal gain. Baai's selfless dedication to various tasks solely out of duty reflected saatvik tyaga, and her life evolved into a spiritual quest for liberation.

3
The Later Phase of Baai's Life

This phase started around 1975 when Baai was about 45–50. Around this time, her eldest son, who had shifted to Pune following his marriage, managed to get a contractual job and was also blessed with a baby boy. Someone was needed to look after the baby, as both parents worked full-time. The dismal situation in Baai's village had not improved much by then.

Considering such circumstances, the family decided that Baai—with her two sons aged 12 and 14—would live with her eldest son so the newborn baby could be cared for. Bhaau was to stay in their village house and visit them periodically in the city. Thus, after making some arrangements for household items such as food grains, flour and fuel wood for Bhaau, and after obtaining transfer certificates from the village school for her two sons, Baai left her village home in Dahigaon to live with her eldest son in Pune.

This move was disruptive for all, especially for Bhaau. He had tremendous affection for his children and could not fathom their absence. His parents had also passed away. In those days, there was a strict division of labour between the male and female members of families in the rural areas. Household chores such as cooking, water-fetching and cleaning were meant to be done by the female members of the family. Thus, Bhaau was not accustomed to cooking, and it was difficult in those days to hire someone who could cook for you.

Furthermore, jobs such as washing one's clothes and utensils, going to the flour mill to get grains milled, or going to a grocery shop to buy cooking oil, would have caused Bhaau some embarrassment and discomfort. More so when gossipmongers in the village may have said that he had been abandoned and neglected by his family members. This role change was particularly awkward in a small village where most people knew each other, and gender roles were orthodox and inflexible. Furthermore, he was still in poor health after the complex abdominal surgery.

∽

Upon arriving in Pune, a new chapter began in Baai's life. So far, she had been one of the main providers of the family's livelihood. Due to Baai's and Bhaau's hard work, the family had achieved some economic stability. So far they had purchased a small piece of agricultural land, run a tailoring shop, educated their eldest son in a town, married off their only daughter at considerable expense, funded their eldest son's transition to Pune after his marriage, covered medical expenses for Baai's father-in-law, provided care and nursing to Baai's ageing parents-in-law, and also managed the expenses of Bhaau's surgery.

In Pune, living in a small rented room with her eldest son's family, Baai was slowly ushered into doing the housework while looking after the newborn grandson. She was relegated to a submissive, servant-like position with no freedom to live on her terms. The living space was crammed with six members in one rented room. Soon, her middle son was admitted to the tenth standard and I (the youngest) to the eighth standard of a school, where we resided in a hostel. Thus, she was separated not only from Bhaau but also from her two sons. However, she rejoiced thinking that her two sons now had access to better education.

Baai's separation from her husband and two sons would have been painful beyond words, as she had devoted most of her life caring for her family members. Also, along with her husband, she was used to sharing considerable agency as the head of the family for several years. And now, she saw herself unexpectedly pushed into a submissive role, having to obey her eldest son and his wife. This shift in Baai's position, at about 45–50, was sudden and unexpected.

∽

The school to which her sons were admitted drew a large proportion of students from slum-like areas around the school rather than from cultured cities. The school was also not known for producing excellent students. The hostel was made available for meagre fees or, for some students, without any fees too. Most of the children in the hostel came from low socio-economic strata, and a few of them used to behave aggressively and showed less interest in education. As Baai's sons had lived in a pious family with devout parents, they found some of their peers quite challenging to be with. The hostel was run by an organization that possibly used the grants received from a charitable society.

The accommodation in the hostel consisted of one large-sized room, two small-sized rooms, and one large rectangular hall. Apart from that, there was a small classroom that could be used for studies in the evening. The three rooms comprised the living space for the students and the large hall was for having food. In each of these rooms, each student was assigned one spot by the wall where he would place his luggage nearly touching the wall. The space of 3–4 ft width and about 6–7 ft length, right in front of the student's trunk, was assigned as 'his space'. This was where a student could sit during the day and sleep during the night. In this arrangement, several students lived and slept side by side in a room. During the day, students used the floor in front of their luggage to sit, to have meals, and to study. At night, students would spread their mats or any other cloth and sleep on it with some cover to pull over. There were no beds or mattresses provided by the hostel. There were a few common bathrooms for the students to use.

Breakfast, lunch and dinner were provided in the hostel. A small kitchen and an adjoining large hall were for meals. Milk, prepared by mixing milk powder with warm water, and also boiled and seasoned lentils, used to be the daily breakfast. The milk powder had a strong, unpleasant odour and did not taste good even after adding sugar to it. Breakfast used to be served around 7.30 a.m. Lunch consisted of a thin curry, made from boiled split pulse and water, and a few pieces of chapati. The chapatis used to be large in size, thick, partly burnt, and partially cooked, possibly due to the hurried cooking done in order to prepare so many pieces of these in a short time. There was also the foul odour of the oil used for cooking them. A limited number of chapatis were provided to each student. Dinner used to be served around 6.00 p.m. and consisted of chapatis and lentil (*moong*) curry. These meals were repeated on a daily basis without any variety. Thus, leafy greens or any other green vegetables, or rice, were never a part of the meals. On a festival day, one *pooran poli* (a sweet item made by filling a sweet paste of boiled split gram and jaggery between two layers of a chapati) used to be served. But even these used to be large, partly burnt and partly raw due to the hurried cooking.

To receive one's meals, one had to carry one's plate and bowl and sit cross-legged in a row on the floor of the hall adjoining the kitchen. One student would then go past each student and place a limited number of chapatis on the student's plate, and another student would pour the curry into the student's plate or bowl. Some students ate their meals while sitting on the hall's floor, while others took their plates to their room and ate it there, sitting at their assigned places next to their trunks.

Adjusting to this new food, shelter and company was difficult for Baai's two sons, particularly for me as the youngest, as I had been highly attached to and dependent on Baai. Possibly due to the type and quality of food and my relatively weak digestive system, I suffered from problems such as abscesses on my head and scabies on my fingers. At home, we were used to having lunch around noon. However, in the hostel, there was a long gap between the lunches, served around 9.30 a.m., and dinners, and we would feel really hungry around noon. Baai realized this and began sending a lunch parcel via a boy who attended the same school and happened to live near the rented room Baai lived in with her eldest son. However, she could send the lunch parcels for not more than a few days, possibly because she sensed a lack of approval of this from her eldest son's family.

This would have caused her tremendous anguish, as she might have been overwhelmed by the sense of helplessness due to her being in a state of dependency.

∽

Some days after the arrival of Baai and her sons in Pune, Bhaau made a brief visit but soon returned to his village. He sent the family a packet of sweets and had another packet delivered to his married daughter who also lived in the same city. It seems that Bhaau did not visit his daughter, as he did not want to cause any inconvenience by turning up at her in-laws' place without an invitation (as was the norm). Travelling to Pune and going back to Dahigaon on the same day would have caused tremendous hardship to him. During his tiring journey, he would have remained without food for more than 24 hours. Five months later (around the period of Deepavali), Bhaau became seriously ill. Baai and her eldest son then travelled from Pune towards Dahigaon. However, on their way, they found Bhaau seated at a bus station in a village close to Dahigaon. Eventually, they brought him to Pune.

There were possibly many reasons for Bhaau's illness. During the period of a few days preceding Deepavali, the custom in Dahigaon was that pious individuals would remain in a temple for seven to eight days and complete the reading of the *Dnyaneshwari* scripture. Such reading of a scripture is referred to as a *paaraayan*. It was learnt that Bhaau had started doing paaraayan in the temple. It is likely that he did not receive proper food during that period, as there was no other family member with him in the village who could have cooked for him. Besides not eating enough, he possibly took cold water baths during those winter days.

His pre-existing long-term ill health condition, inadequate care and nourishment during the five–six months since his family's departure for Pune, his emotional turmoil from living alone in Dahigaon, and inadequate food intake during the scripture-reading period are likely to have been some of the factors leading to Bhaau's deteriorating health. So, by the time Baai and her eldest son brought him to Pune, his health had taken a serious turn and he had to be admitted to a public hospital for out-patient treatment. Tragically, within a few days of him being brought to Pune, Bhaau passed away.

This was a terrible blow to Baai. Later, Baai said that she continued to live just for her children's sake, knowing that they needed their mother around them. She continued to maintain her existence as a service to others. Her stay with her eldest son's family in Pune did not give her any relief. For example, she would have to fetch water for the entire family, which required carrying water-filled pitchers on her head from a public water tap to the house. She had to wash all the clothes of the family, scour and clean utensils, sweep the floor as well as cook for the family, apart from taking care of her grandsons. She provided great care to her two grandsons while accepting the loss of her agency. Such a pattern continued for about 10 years.

∽

Around 1983, Baai's middle son got married, and his family lived with the eldest son's family for some time in what was now a larger house. A couple of years after marriage, he relocated with his family into a separate flat, some distance away, although still in the city of Pune.

Baai moved with her middle son to look after his newborn son. However, her leaving her eldest son's home caused some unhappiness to his family. Both Baai's middle son and his wife were employed and hence someone was required at home to look after their newborn son, and also their daughter who was born a few years later. Baai provided her usual dedication and love while rearing these two grandchildren.

In this flat, her physical hardship was reduced because water was available at home and there was house help to do the sweeping, scouring and cleaning of utensils, and some amount of cooking. This gave her enough time to affectionately rear her two grandchildren. For example, she would take them to and get them back from their nursery school. She would also lovingly massage them using coconut oil, before giving them a bath, and spend quite some time preparing tasty but simple, special dishes for her grandchildren. She would make nice laddus for her grandson to eat, as he relished those. When they grew up a little, she would take them for walks and to sit in some open and airy space in the evening hours. She involved herself in child-rearing with dedication and love while accepting submissiveness, loss of self-reliance, and loss of freedom in decision-making.

Baai had not been able to attend school due to her impoverished circumstances; therefore she could not read or write and hence could not even read scriptures. As she had some time at her disposal while living with her middle son and his family, Baai got associated with a woman who could read. The woman would read out the scriptures, and Baai would listen. The relief from household work and the availability of time were used by her to educate herself. So, around the age of 65, Baai began her self-schooling at home and learnt the English alphabet. Soon, she mastered writing simple words and learnt to sign on her own too.

Having acquired reading skills, Baai read *Hari Paath*. It is a collection of devotional lyrics composed by various saints that glorify God, describe the importance of devotion, advise continually maintaining God's remembrance and chanting God's holy name, and recommend leading a virtuous and altruistic life. Thereafter, till the day she left her physical body, she used to continually recite the Hari Paath on a daily basis. Thus, through reading, she developed a new form of devotion to and connectedness with God at the age of about 65.

∽

Around that period, I went to the United States (US) to undertake my doctoral studies. While I was gathering funds, Baai felt sad that she did not have the capacity to provide any help for my higher education journey. She compensated for this by offering daily prayers for the successful completion of my doctoral studies. Baai also did paaraayan of a scripture named Nav Naath—meaning nine great saints (from the yogic sect Naath Panthis) who had acquired a high spiritual level through several austerities, and lived an austere and renounced life—with an accompanying prayer. Her prayer was: just as one of the main saints in the scripture, Machindranath Ji Maharaj—who was accidentally trapped in an inappropriate illusion-filled place, and was later brought back from there by his disciple—her youngest son too should be brought back from the land of dreams (that the US was known to be) to his own country India.

While studying for my doctorate, I received inspiration, protection and positive outcomes in a miraculous manner at some important stages, despite being far away in a different continent. This was a result of Baai's prayers and blessings. After all, blessings and facilitation through prayers work without the constraints of time and space. At some critical moments in my doctoral studies, I would speak to Baai on the phone, remember her, or simply request her blessings in prayers.

As I penned the dedication for my doctoral dissertation, words flowed in an unplanned manner onto the page, revealing that the foundation of my educational journey was rooted in the enduring influence of Baai and Bhaau, and that this dissertation was dedicated to them. Their resilience, sacrifices and unwavering morality served as my guiding light, inspiring me to pursue knowledge with gratitude and dedication. This dedication was not deliberate, but the result of a divine realization that dawned on me. During four-and-a-half years of separation from Baai, I had become quite weak and exhausted. Upon returning to India, I touched Baai's feet to pay obeisance to her, placed a copy of my thesis in her hands, and told her that it was dedicated to her. She looked at it, and also at my emaciated and weakened body, and shed tears. She was then living with the family of one of her married sons and was dependent on him. Hence, she could not take any initiative in providing special care to me. She took me to an Ayurvedic doctor who provided me with medicines.

My doctoral journey had made me somewhat inward-focused and reticent, in sharp contrast to my talkative and reasonably outgoing younger self. Having noticed this shift, Baai advised me on various aspects of life, such as how to get over one's childhood mistakes, how to avoid dwelling on the past, and how to remain in the present and work towards the future. Even though she was old and lacked financial independence and agency, she continued to fulfil her family duties by providing sound advice to me when I was about 33.

She had a subtle way of sharing her wisdom and advising others on solving various life problems. Rather than taking on the role of a solution-provider, Baai would indirectly provide advice by drawing on analogies, proverbs, parables, mythological stories, real-life examples, hypothetical examples, and also preaching from the holy scriptures. She intuitively understood that I had become quite inward-focused and had been feeling sad about some trivial events from the past. Rather than telling me about her observations directly, she explained things indirectly through various conversations. For example, she said that as a river flows by retaining clear water on its surface and leaves behind grime and dirt, so too one should leave behind and not repeatedly recall the sad events of one's life.

She added that when one cleans grains using a sieve, the small particles of soil and dirt fall through, while the grains remain in the sieve. Similarly, one should leave behind sad memories and retain the positive memories of one's life.

Using yet another analogy, she said that in order to write new letters on a slate, the old letters need to be erased. In other words, one is required to keep aside one's past in order to live in the present. While providing these words of wisdom, she showed much affection through her voice, gaze and gestures.

She went on to cite an example outlining the adverse consequences of overthinking and getting carried away by one's thoughts. In one example, Baai said that a worm named *bhinguti* (chrysalis) creates a shell around its body, gets encased inside the shell, then cannot break the shell, and eventually dies within it. Similarly, one should not get so immersed in one's thoughts that it constrains one's functioning, and one gets locked up within the web of beliefs created by one's own thinking. While narrating this example, she did not tell me that I had a tendency to create a web of thoughts that constrained my functioning. This intuitive way of observing others, sensing their spiritual or existential problems, and gently providing them helpful solutions in a subtle way was her unobtrusive style of helping others.

Baai also realized that, as part of my spiritual journey, I was following too many restrictions, including on food intake. As a result, I was missing out on essential nutrients. She then narrated to me the example of a saint who used to perform his prayers after meals, saying that it is not necessary to deprive oneself of food in order to practise devotion to God. She also lovingly explained that there is a living element of God (*jeeva* or *aatma*) within each creature and hence one should not cause distress to that living element by depriving the body of necessary nutrition and rest.

Indeed, the holy scriptures such as *Dnyaneshwari* and Sant Shri Tukaram Ji Maharaj's collection of abhangas named *Gatha* also provide similar advice. For example, one abhanga of Shri Tukaram Ji Maharaj[1] advises not to cut down on food and not to be isolated from the world by going to forests, but to engage in God's remembrance while living in society. Another abhanga of Shri Tukaram Ji Maharaj mentions that he did not engage in austerities nor constricted his mind, but rendered service to God only through remembrance of God[2]. Shrimad Bhagavad Gita suggests that union with God (yoga) is not attainable to those who eat too little and those who do not maintain a balance in their intake[3]. The Gita also suggests that the austerities that cause distress or pain to one's body are in the mode of ignorance (*tamas tapa*)[4]. Thus, some of the advice provided by Baai came from her high level of spiritual development and her innate knowledge or discovery of some vital spiritual principles.

Baai used to mention practically useful proverbs in order to help me constrain my idealism and enhance my practical mindset. For example, she used to say, 'If one's mind is well then one can attain great things (*Maan hai changa to kathwat me ganga*).' Another one she mentioned was 'one may listen to others, but one should follow one's conscience (*aikaawe janaache, karaawe manaache*),' and also 'people ridicule any action one takes (*lok ghodyavar basu det naahit, aani khaali chaalu det naahit*).' In other words, one should not pay much attention to people's remarks about one's actions but simply do the right thing.

She also noticed that I used to feel sad even at a small deviation from moral norms such as truth, non-violence and altruism. I would then try to make up for this through penance (*praayschitta*) as a form of self-imposed punishment for the deviation. She once narrated a parable that a person was having his meal when a fly fell in his food and died. He felt the need to perform a penance for the fly's death, so he went to a river to perform the penance of a cold-water bath. As he took water in his palms, he saw an insect that was dying in it. Then he felt the need to do another penance, and the cycle continued. After performing a series of unending penances, he remained hungry throughout the day and could not go back and have his meal. In other words, carrying out too many acts of penance could be a futile process, particularly when the perceived trivial deviations were the creations of one's own, and possibly restrictive, beliefs.

Baai also used to tell me that one should make one's mind steady and not allow it to flit, which is also one of the important goals of spiritual refinement mentioned by various saints. For example, Sant Shri Eknath Ji Maharaj mentions in one of his abhangas[5] that doing one's routine and incidental deeds purify the mind, and practising devotion to God or engaging the mind in God (*upaasana*) makes the mind steady. Similarly, Sant Shri Dnyaneshwar Ji's abhanga[6] mentions that one who goes after his mind is lost, but the one who steadies his mind on God is the blessed one.

In this phase of life, Baai's sense of duty, acceptance, perseverance, concern for others, selflessness, spirit of sacrifice, and devotion to God remained steadfast. She demonstrated a sense of acceptance and equanimity in the face of several painful happenings, such as the untimely death of her husband at the age of about 50, and her significant shift to a peripheral role in the changing family pattern. By 1998, she had become old and attained the age of about 70–75.

GLEANINGS

- Baai adopted additional forms of connecting with God facilitated by her new circumstances and capabilities, as exemplified in her newly adopted routine of reading the Hari Paath daily, thanks to her newly acquired literacy.
- Baai's long history of discharging her responsibilities as God-ordained duties and maintaining a continual connection with God—reflecting a connection with God through work and devotion (karma yoga and bhakti yoga)—possibly facilitated her spiritual development and gave her spiritual wisdom, and also made Baai's advice at par with that of evolved saints and with what is written in the scriptures.

4

The Old-Age Phase of Baai's Life

Around 1998, just after earning my doctorate, I faced certain difficulties in my personal life. Baai moved in with me to provide affection and care during this difficult period. So, at the age of about 70–75, she faced the altogether new challenge of protecting her youngest son from trauma, and helping him with her sage-like advice, wisdom and affection. Given that she was such a pillar of strength to those around her, just as her shifting from her eldest son's house to the middle son's house had caused unhappiness to the former, so did her shifting in with me cause some unhappiness to the middle son. This unhappiness possibly undermined the family's appreciation for the service that she had rendered them.

My pursuit of higher education and extremely strenuous hard work for the doctorate degree from the US was largely inspired by my early childhood impressions of the great desire my parents had for their children's education. I was also inspired by my early childhood memories of the efforts, determination and perseverance Baai and Bhaau had exhibited through seemingly insurmountable hardships, and also the sacrifices they had made for the education and bright future of their children. As mentioned previously, my intense dedication to doctoral studies took its toll, rendering me physically weak, emotionally fragile, and spiritually inclined by the age of 33. I believe that at that time my spiritual quest was not adequately informed, and also that there was a lack of integration between my spiritual endeavours and my relational, social, economic and professional sides. My spiritual journey was painful to me, and when Baai lived with me, she too suffered by witnessing my suffering.

∽

As I did not have a family of my own and had adopted an austere lifestyle as a part of my spiritual journey, Baai was deprived of a comfortable family life that would have been provided by a daughter-in-law. Thus, in her old age, she did not receive the kind of care from a female family member that she herself had provided to her in-laws in their old age. She must also have felt the pain of separation from her grandchildren, whom she had nourished and cared for. But she suffered in silence so as not to upset me. During a period of about 18–19 years from 1998 to 2017, Baai lived either with me or alone in my flat in Pune, which was home for both of us and where we used to live together whenever I was in Pune either for my employment or during my long summer vacation. During the first seven years, we moved to different locations while I was exploring a suitable place of work. This deprived her of the stability required in old age.

While working in Pune, I once travelled to a distant place in 2006 to explore an employment opportunity. When I returned, Baai understood from my expressions that I had taken a liking to that place of employment, which was about 1,000 km from Pune, in a region with a different climate, language and culture. Baai was about 78–83 years old then and had become fragile in mind and body. Even though it meant getting disconnected from Pune and from her relatives, she decided to move with me for my happiness. After a long train journey of about 30 hours, we reached the venue only to find that the weather conditions and food available there were quite different. Baai clearly suffered there in many ways, while trying to adjust. As usual, she never complained, nor did she show any gesture of suffering. Instead, she got immersed in her duties of supporting me. However, after about two to three months, I realized that her stay in that location was not suitable for her. Thus, I went back with her to Pune and arranged for her to stay in my small flat, while I returned to my place of work.

She had to live alone in Pune from 2006. Thus, in this later stage of her life, she had to initially sacrifice permanence and stability, and later live alone. Living alone in old age must have been painful for a person who had spent most of her life nurturing various families. However, as always, she accepted this situation with a sense of equanimity.

Facing the loss of physical capacity for doing productive work, and also experiencing loneliness, Baai worked to make her faith in God even more firm and her devotion even more intense. She offered all her past efforts, struggles, sacrifices, contributions to the family, and accomplishments as offerings to God. She relinquished the sense of being the doer of her deeds and accomplishments. She no longer desired good outcomes from the good deeds she had performed in the service of all her family members and several others over the last few decades. She frequently told herself that God got all the good deeds done through her, while she offered those good deeds at the feet of God without expecting any sensual or worldly reward from them.

In turn, Baai was blessed with God's immense grace, manifested through various forms: the realization of God's presence within her being, an experiential encounter with the divine, a profound awareness that God resides within every being and form, and a deep sense of peace, contentment and patience as she awaited the ultimate call from God's abode. Baai was at peace and had no need to search for God in a temple or on a pilgrimage. Rather, her every deed from then onwards was in the service of maintaining her union with God. With her profound experience of realizing God, she no longer needed to engage in God's pursuit. In other words, she had already reached the destination.

∽

So, at the age of about 80, Baai lived a life away from the very family members she had nourished, served and loved, including the children she had cared for and protected from harm as much as possible. In this solitary phase, one of the first things Baai did was that she obtained an earthen pot (*kundi*), soil and a basil (*tulsi*) sapling, and using these items she planted the sapling in the balcony of her small flat. The basil plant is regarded as holy in India and watering this plant daily, and paying obeisance to it, is considered to be an expression of one's devotion to God.

Baai also requested a local carpenter to make a small *devghar* (a case or shelf to keep the holy images representing various deities for daily worship) out of simple wooden planks that were available with him. Thus, a simple box-shaped devghar got installed in her bedroom. She would water the tulsi plant while doing her prayers every morning after her bath. Thereafter, she would proceed to perform the worship of the deities (*dev pooja*) in her devghar. She would remain deeply absorbed in thoughts of God while performing her morning worship, as though she was at her eternal destination and hence not in haste to go anywhere.

Her day would start at about 6.00 a.m. with bathing and other cleaning work. Then, she would water and worship the tulsi plant in her balcony, and sit to perform morning japa and prayers. After the morning worship, she would recite the Hari Paath. She had her small-sized copy of the same in the form of a booklet, and she had memorized most of the couplets in it over time.

She would take a simple breakfast consisting of a bhaakari and some simple curry. Her meals were taken care of by the same woman who would do the house-cleaning work. Before having breakfast, she would thank God for having provided food for her, offer it to God, and then take the first morsel. After breakfast, she would again thank God for having provided her food and satiated her hunger. She would then wash her breakfast utensils and do some tidying-up work in the kitchen area, as she would always maintain tidiness around her. For each meal of the day, she would follow the pattern of commencing and ending the meal by praying to God. Occasionally, while lying on bed at night, she would fold her hands in prayer.

After breakfast, she would take some rest and then take a stroll in the front side of the housing society complex in which the small flats were located. She would also sit for some time on one of the benches in the small seating area, meant mostly for the elderly residents of the society.

There, she would talk to a few women and understand their concerns, difficulties and sorrows.

As per her way of living—without taking the role of a preacher, counsellor or even of a guide—she would mention the related proverbs and narrate stories that would aim at healing them. Her empathy-filled presence, affectionate smile, selfless orientation, wisdom and peace-filled existence itself became a source of peace and happiness to the women around her. Hence, several women usually gathered around her on a daily basis.

Then, she would return to her small flat and lie down for a while. She would have a light lunch consisting of bhaakari and curry between 1.00 and 2.00 p.m., clean her lunch utensils, and tidy up the kitchen before her afternoon nap. She would get up around 4.00 p.m., and then gather some women from her housing society for singing abhangas or doing *bhajan*s (singing devotional songs, usually in a group). She would sing in her mellow voice while teaching the women how to sing in rhythm. She had memorized all the words in several abhangas. At times, she would go into a trance-like state while singing.

With the help of the women, a comprehensive collection of abhangas was put together in Baai's notebook. After the singing sessions, which went on for about two hours, some items such as fruit, puffed rice, sugar, or small portions of delicious but simple homemade food items would be distributed as *prasaad* (holy offerings). Thereafter, the women would discuss their household or personal matters. These discussions would cover happenings of joy and sorrow in their households or in their personal lives, changes, illnesses, grievances, domestic difficulties, accomplishments, and many such things associated with family life. During such discussions, Baai continued to offer advice by using simple words that would give solutions, guidance, hope, courage and comfort to others. The women came to love, respect and even adore Baai.

After singing abhangas, she was able to immediately turn her attention to the problems that the women were facing in their worldly life. Her ability to quickly switch from a transcendental or spiritual state to a more worldly or material one was remarkable. Improving worldly life while upholding high ethical standards was to her a way of fulfilling her God-ordained duties, and thereby a way of practising devotion to God. Also, she had the capacity to listen to and address worldly problems of others, as she realized that God resides in every form of life and that serving human beings by addressing their problems and providing solutions was itself a service and devotion to God.

During the bhajan sessions, Baai would take great care in neatly organizing the things used. For example, after a session she would neatly tie the cymbals used. She would also prepare her house tidily before the beginning of the bhajan, and neatly spread a cloth or mat on the floor for women to sit on. Thus, for her, every deed in the material world had an aspect of divinity in it. In other words, for her there was a link between the material aspects and the transcendental or divine aspects.

In the evenings, Baai would perform her japa while being seated in front of the devghar. Then she would perform her *aarati* and pray. As she was about 80–85 years old by then, she would often feel weary after exerting herself in such endeavours. Thus, after her evening prayers, she would lie down to rest. Then she would have dinner at around 8.00 p.m. Most days her dinner consisted of the same food items as in her breakfast and lunch. On the whole, her meals used to be simple, frugal and health-preserving. Baai used to say that one should look after one's health and keep it in good condition so that one does not later blame God for any ill health. She used to feel satiated and grateful at the end of her meals. It was God's grace that she used to derive contentment and happiness from such simple meals.

After completing dinner, she would wash her dinner utensils and clean the kitchen. Then she would climb down the staircase of about 14 steps from her flat on the first floor to the front yard of the society where she would sit on one of the benches. While seated, she would listen to other women's concerns, comforting them, guiding them and helping them. After about an hour of such social service, she would again climb the stairs to reach her flat, and then sleep at about 10.00 p.m.

Baai also organized various spiritual and religious activities. At times, she organized daily sessions of paaraayan. After certain days of such daily, non-stop reading, when the entire scripture reading was complete, a small community meal would be arranged. During those scripture-reading sessions, she would occasionally explain—in a simple and unassuming manner—the meaning of some intriguing or complex text in the scripture. Surprisingly, though Baai had not received any formal education, she used to explain the essence of the scripture to other educated women, probably drawing from her experience of God.

As a way of providing pure (saatvik) form of happiness

to others, Baai would also organize some community feasts on auspicious occasions or days of religious significance such as *champa-shashti*. These feasts would be arranged as a collaborative activity with efforts from several women. Each woman would bring some ingredients for preparing various food items while others would cook them in the kitchen at Baai's flat. Others would bring a few already-cooked food items to be included as a part of the feast. After the cooking was completed, some spiritual activities such as reading a scripture or singing devotional lyrics or prayers would be collectively performed. Thereafter, some food items would be offered to God. Then, all women would eat the meal prepared in the special feast.

Baai also provided affection, care and guidance to the children of her neighbour's family. The parents would feel quite relieved if they had to travel for a couple of days or so while leaving their young children at home because Baai would provide the required attention and care to the children, while also ensuring they maintained their daily routine in the absence of their parents.

∽

She maintained fairness in her dealings with others. As she stayed alone in her old age, she needed many forms of support from others, such as ordering a cylinder for cooking gas, buying groceries or medicine, or receiving help in preparing some homemade remedy for minor health problems such as a cold or body ache. She would always try to reciprocate in some way to those who offered her such assistance.

Many people said that when they entered Baai's small flat, they would experience the same peace that they experienced when entering a temple. When I would travel from my distant employment place to visit her in Pune, I too would experience a distinct serenity and bliss in her flat. Possibly, her faith in God, and thereby the peace she achieved, radiated from her and spread to her surroundings. This was possibly the reason why several people used to get attracted to and spend time with Baai.

Baai spoke affectionately to everyone. She spoke with concern and affection, offering soothing words to all, even to those relatives who had been unjust to her in some ways. She would say that a river allows a cow and a tiger alike to drink its water and quench their thirst, and in the same way she would provide the same affection to all without discriminating. She also used to say that she had forgiven all people in her life. She did not bear any ill-feelings towards anyone and did not speak harshly to anyone. Throughout her life, the circumstances and misdeeds of others, which would ordinarily have invoked a harsh response from anyone else in her place, were responded to by her with patience, endurance and equanimity.

Baai realized that providing happiness to all and avoiding deliberate harm is itself a service to God. This manifested in her in various altruistic forms for enhancing the well-being of all. For example, after the end of summer months, when rains would start, she would look to the sky and say, 'Oh, rain, please do come so that the green leaves will grow on the trees, green grass blades will be available as food (*anna–paani, chaara*) for animals and birds (*pashu–pakshi*), and so that farmers can sow their fields and cultivate them to get crops as food for all.' However, if it rained untimely, Baai would express her sorrow and say, 'Oh, now the mango fruits and other crops of the farmers may be damaged.' Thus, she prayed and implored the rains to come timely so that the requirements of food and water for farmers, birds and animals were fulfilled.

She accepted the unfolding ageing process while she awaited the eventual call of God for her eternal destination. Baai used to say that only God knew when God would take her to heaven. She never used the word 'death', but rather spoke about being taken or carried by God to the heavenly abode (*devaaghari*). She used to suffer from pain in her old age, including acute pain in her legs, palms and fingers too. The pain used to be more severe in winters and monsoons. Acknowledging the pain, she would express that given the extensive physical labour she had undertaken throughout her life, experiencing pain in old age was unavoidable. In this way, she exhibited a degree of detachment from her body and bodily pains.

∽

I used to visit Baai typically twice a year. For the festival of Deepavali, I would visit her for about a week, and then in the summer I would visit her for two months from mid-April until mid-June. I started noticing that she was getting old and frail, and that it was not appropriate for her to live alone at that age. I explored various options to find a suitable place of employment close to Pune but was unable to find anything. One day, after my evening prayers, I expressed my worry and sadness at not being able to be with her in her hour of need. To this, she advised me to focus on my academic work, adding that she was looking after herself well and did not feel lonely. She assured me that I would get the opportunity to render in-person service to her when she needed it.

When I returned to the distant town of my work for quite some period of time, I used to phone her almost every evening. When she spoke on the phone, she seemed to make a deliberate effort to sound well and to provide an impression that she was in good health in order to prevent me from feeling concerned about her and getting distracted from my work. However, the weakness of the aged body, low energy levels, and signs of fatigue and tiredness became increasingly noticeable when she spoke on the phone. Baai would say that God looked after her and protected her. When asked if she was not worried about living alone when her body was becoming increasingly weak, she said she would manage her life to the extent that her body allowed her to, and thereafter it was '*Raam Krishna Hari*'—in other words, God would take care of her and her fate would be decided as per God's wish.

Baai recalled that some of her aspirations in her childhood were very simple and that those aspirations had been fulfilled. For example, she said that her childhood dream was to have a cow and a few she-goats at the house. Despite having moved from a rural to an urban area, and from having been in poverty for a considerable period to later experiencing a reasonable standard of living in middle age and some prosperity of her children, she had retained an awareness of her humble circumstances in the early period of her life, while also continuing to remain satisfied with life and grateful to God.

Thus, she had lived the active years of her ordinary life in a noble, pious and altruistic manner, and maintained a connection with God through various forms of devotion. In old age, she experienced freedom from cravings and hence was at peace. While her frail body meant that she could no longer exert physical effort for the well-being of others, she continued working to enhance their well-being through her prayers.

> **GLEANINGS**
>
> - Baai had lost her cravings, and developed a sense of detachment from her body and bodily sufferings of old age, possibly because she had reached the state of liberation (*mukti*).
> - One of Sant Tukaram Ji's abhangas[1] reflects such a way of living and its outcome. It mentions that his strivings throughout his life were in the service of making the last day of life sweet. This led to the extinction of cravings or desires and the attainment of peace for him. He was, thus, in the state of liberation and spent his last few days in happiness.
> - Baai's concern for the well-being of others was not limited to her family members, relatives and acquaintances, but it also got extended to others such as farmers, birds and animals, etc. This orientation of being engaged in the well-being of all, referred to as '*sarva bhute hita-rataah*' in the scriptures, is a means to, or a requirement for, self-realization and liberation.[2] Her concern for the well-being of all, including birds and animals, reflected her awareness of the harmony of all forms of existence. Such awareness is a characteristic of transcendence as discussed in the scientific literature on spirituality[3].

5

Baai's Declining Health and Her Journey towards Her Eternal Abode

In the summer of 2013, at the age of about 85–90, Baai suffered a health episode, and she felt difficulty breathing. Medical treatment, including a couple of days of hospitalization at a nearby clinic, gave her some relief. At that time, I was with her, anxious about leaving her alone, as I was obliged to return to my workplace. I managed to persuade her to stay at my brother's place, to which she reluctantly agreed. Thereafter, I travelled back to my workplace.

A few months later, I learnt that Baai had not been able to adjust well to the shift, and had become weak and quiet. As I was about 1,000 km away, I could not return immediately. Thus, I tried to speak to some people in Pune in order to shift her to her original place of living. But these efforts did not succeed. A few weeks later, I learnt that her health had further deteriorated, and I immediately set off for Pune. Upon reaching Pune, I found her in an extremely ill state and came to know that she had had a fall. She could not get down from bed or walk on her own, and her speech also had become impaired. Even in this condition, she affectionately acknowledged my arrival and touched me with love. Medical reports revealed that she had suffered a hairline fracture in the waist. The very next day, I shifted her back to my flat, met the orthopaedic surgeon who had given the initial treatment for her fracture, discussed her situation with my siblings, and, thinking that Baai would recover with the ongoing treatment and my siblings' coordinated attention, returned to my distant place of work.

However, the arrangement for the treatment and care of Baai did not work out well, and her health did not seem to improve. Even in that situation, she wished not to cause any inconvenience to anyone and hence she herself tried to give the impression that her health was alright. Her daughter had come to care for her for some time. Once, during Baai's telephonic conversation with me, I asked if she could pass the phone to my sister. I overheard her telling my sister, 'Please do not tell him that I am unwell, otherwise he will leave his work and come here to look after me.' Thus, even in an extremely serious health condition, she cared for others, avoided any inconvenience to others, and helped others to do their own work and live their own life in a manner that would make them happy. Though she was in a serious state of ill health and had become a bit incoherent, she made deliberate efforts to stay alert the moment I expressed concern.

From her speech during the telephonic conversation, I sensed that her health condition was serious, and so I immediately began the journey back to Pune again. Her ill-health situation had indeed become more complex. She had a hairline fracture at her waist, she could not walk or stand, and had to be placed in a chair with assistance. Also, her speech was impaired, her comprehension was somewhat incoherent, she had difficulty breathing, and she had an acute cough that was later diagnosed as pneumonia.

∽

One afternoon, Baai's daughter and others requested her to sing an abhanga. Despite her serious ill health and difficulty in breathing and speaking, she accepted the request because she never wanted to disappoint anyone. She was helped out of bed and was placed on a chair with pillows for her back. A shawl was wrapped around her chest, and a pair of cymbals was placed in her hands. She started her bhajan session with the customary loud, repetitive chanting of God's name—*Jaya Jaya Raam Krishna Hari*—and then went on to sing the customary opening abhanga. She was intermittently having bouts of cough, and she had to make deliberate and painful efforts to breathe.

Soon, Baai's voice became strong, the energy level became higher, her words had far more clarity than before, and she could even sing the entire set of couplets in each of the devotional lyrics with only occasional corrections required. Within a few minutes, she began to go into a state of deep trance while singing. As her mind got connected to and immersed in the divine, she almost became oblivious to her body's ill health. Her painful symptoms, breathing difficulties, incoherence and even weakness diminished as she sang in a state of divine bliss.

Baai concluded her bhajan session by reciting *pasaayadaan* (a prayer attributed to Sant Shri Dnyaneshwar Maharaj Ji) seeking God's blessings for the elimination of vices, the development of virtues, the inspiration of noble deeds, the fostering of harmony, the eradication of ignorance, and the realization of one's duties among all creatures. Thereafter, she repeatedly chanted *'Jaya Jaya Raam Krishna Hari'* and ended with a prayer of Sant Shri Ramdas Swami—a prayer for continual union with the divine, and for the use of one's body in the service of the divine.

This transformation of her state during the bhajan—her energetic singing, her immersion in devotion to God, her elevation to a state of trance, and her being oblivious to her body's pain and limitations—were all indications of Baai's detachment from her body, her connection to the divine, her union with God, and the experience of a state of liberation from the physical body, referred to as *muktaavastha* or *mokshasthiti*. Thus, her spiritual evolution had reached a stage where she could attain yoga in the form of union or oneness with God.

∽

Over the next few days, Baai's cough did not subside with the ongoing treatment, and further medical investigations were done. These revealed that she had pneumonia and may have suffered a stroke. She was hospitalized when doctors discovered an electrolyte imbalance as well in her. After a few days of treatment, she recovered from pneumonia and returned home. Her other problems such as the hairline fracture in her waist, the resulting inability to walk or stand, impaired speech, and some incoherence in thought and speech continued to trouble her.

One day, Baai felt uneasy and complained about pain in her abdominal and chest parts. A doctor from a nearby clinic examined her at home and said it was nothing serious, besides her already present physical problems. However, a couple of days later, her alertness noticeably reduced and a huge swelling appeared on her legs. Another doctor paid a home visit and indirectly hinted at the futility of hospitalizing Baai or providing any elaborate treatment to her due to a natural deterioration in her condition as a result of old age.

As Baai's health continued to worsen, another doctor was called in and he opined that she should be immediately hospitalized. Thus, she was rushed to a small nearby hospital and within a few hours of admission, was transferred to a larger hospital. The doctor there diagnosed that she had had a stroke, suffered a heart attack, and been having problems of atrial fibrillation too. A few days later, she was also diagnosed as having skeletal tuberculosis. In such a condition, her legs and arms became so swollen that it was difficult for her to move.

She was subsequently admitted to the ICU, as her condition became critical. She was on heavy medication and had not taken a proper meal for quite a few days by then. As was customary, several relatives visited her. I tried to remain by Baai's bedside in the ICU as much as possible, within the restrictive access rules of the ICU.

When Baai's middle daughter-in-law visited her, she knew from her past experiences that I might not engage in the customary courtesies of asking about her welfare. So she took the initiative to speak with her before going into a partly unconscious state. A few moments later, however, she asked me whether I had spoken with her daughter-in-law. Thus, as was customary with Baai, her concern about providing happiness and avoiding pain for others was exhibited even when she was in the ICU, at a time when her health was in an extremely precarious condition.

One of her grandsons and his wife also came to see Baai in the ICU. While they spoke, she recognized them. As her arms had become heavy and swollen, and were plastered with thin layers of bandages, it was not possible for her to lift her hands. Thus, she asked me to lift her hand so that she could place it on top of her grandson's head as a customary gesture of bestowing blessings. Such was her presence of mind even when her body was painfully weak and wracked with pain. As soon as Baai became a little more alert in the ICU, she even reached out to enquire about the welfare of the family of a lady security guard at the ICU, who had confided in Baai about her family problems.

After a few days of treatment in the ICU, Baai was shifted to the general in-patient ward. Heavy medication and ill health continued. For her, the right treatment was not always feasible due to her old age (about 90 years). For example, a cardiologist opined that the required surgery for Baai's heart problems was not feasible because of her old age. Further, her low alertness, and sometimes even loss of consciousness, made it difficult to provide certain medicines to her. Her food intake was considerably reduced for some time and her sleep cycle was disturbed. She would sleep during the day and remain awake at night.

After having been hospitalized for about a month, Baai's health condition improved to some extent and she was discharged. Once back at home, her health condition gradually improved. I brought some ayurvedic oil to massage her legs and arms, which were affected because of the stroke. I also regularly took her out in a wheelchair, so she could experience the pleasure of seeing the sky, trees, flowers, birds and people. I also explored ways of providing the required nourishment through items such as milk, dates, prunes and figs. New gowns were stitched for Baai to make her feel fresh, and new glass bangles were put around her wrists because her old bangles were either broken or had been removed during her hospital treatment. Also, a couple of delicacies were ordered so that she could eat some tasty items. I got a fresh coat of paint done for Baai's flat. I guess these actions came from the realization that we had nearly lost her.

∽

Over the next few months, she recovered and gradually began to walk with the aid of a walker, and later, she began walking with just the support of a cane. By that time, I had been away from work for about four months in order to be with her during her ill health, treatment and recovery. As it did not seem to be appropriate to shift Baai out of Pune, I decided to explore options in or close to Pune, so as to provide her the close attention and care required. As my workplace had kindly provided me leave without pay during my mother's treatment, I felt obliged to first resume work, and only then explore job options. So I returned to work in early 2014, and then began to explore the job options. It was necessary for some family members to be present with Baai during her post-recovery period, but somehow no family member came forward.

She again had to live alone. She received help from a neighbour's family, who agreed to look after her for some monetary exchange. Even in her poor health, she encouraged me to return to my distant workplace, assuring me that she could manage by herself during the post-recovery period. Every day, when I would call to enquire about her, she would deliberately speak in an energetic manner, assuring me that all was well. To any query about her health, she would promptly respond by saying she was fine (*chaangali aahe*).

In about eight weeks' time, I managed to obtain an employment option about 500 km away from Pune, which meant I could travel overnight to meet Baai. As the weather conditions and food there were somewhat similar to that of Pune, it was possible to shift her to that place without causing any undue hardship to her.

For the next 10 months or so (till early February 2015) Baai stayed under various arrangements, including at our Pune flat for about three months, with her daughter for a couple of months, and with her middle son for a few weeks. She then returned to our flat, where she lived alone for about five months with the help of a part-time housemaid. The maid would cook the food, clean the house, bathe Baai, and wash her clothes. She did not feel or express any sense of bitterness, sadness or anxiety about being constantly shifted.

This recovery phase was not without its hardships. Once, she developed a painful boil on her foot. On another occasion, she had an aching tooth. As I could visit her only once a week or so, she would wait for me to arrive and then tell me about any health problem she had, like her toothache. I only discovered upon meeting her that her toothache was so intense that she couldn't chew anything. Consequently, she resorted to soaking a portion of bhaakari in boiling water and then adding jaggery to make it palatable for chewing. The dentist advised extraction of the tooth that was causing the pain. However, as she was taking blood-thinning tablets for her cardiac illness, a physician advised against the tooth extraction because the blood-thinning medication could possibly lead to excessive bleeding during her tooth extraction. But Baai didn't complain, and she continued to bear the pain of the aching tooth with endurance and a sense of acceptance until it gradually diminished.

During this period, I took Baai to a holy place of pilgrimage in Alandi village. This place of pilgrimage is sanctified mainly because Sant Shri Dnyaneshwar Ji Maharaj took samadhi there. She was taken for a personal *darshan* (having a sight of or paying obeisance to the deities or other holy symbols), and then also attended the afternoon discourse that took place in the temple hall.

Baai was extremely serene and at peace throughout this pilgrimage. Her lack of any desperation to search for God came from her having already experienced God. Her continual and uninterrupted connection with God in her thoughts, feelings and actions throughout her life had provided her the realization that God was within oneself. Thus, she did not need to start or do a search for God anymore, and she did not long for any benefit from a pilgrimage. This was unlike many elderly people who would often go on a frantic search for God in temples or by going on pilgrimages.

∽

In early 2015, I started a new job in Pune, and thus her phase of living alone came to an end. She continued to experience some minor ailments. For instance, when she had a cold, a neighbour helped her by administering steam inhalation using a sizeable vessel filled with boiling water. Once, the container somehow got tilted and the boiled water fell on Baai's leg, inflicting a large burn on her skin. The burn remained serious for several days and she had to suffer the pain, get taken to multiple doctors, take medicines, and also go through the pain of periodical dressing of the wound. Another time, she had a fall in the bathroom and her head hit the wall, leading to injury in the form of a mild subdural haematoma. The dullness and haziness remained for a few weeks until her internal injury healed on its own.

During this period, Baai resumed her afternoon bhajan sessions, in which women from neighbouring families would gather in her bedroom and sing abhangas. She also resumed her practice of reciting Hari Paath every morning. In the period following her recovery, Baai continued to speak affectionately and caringly to her three sons and daughter, with their families, with other relatives, and with everyone else from the community. When any of her sons' families held any function and invited her to their house, she would exude extra energy while getting ready. She did not want others to feel unhappy about her frail state and hence made deliberate efforts to project that she was energetic and well. She would selectively eat food items suitable for her health with contentment, bless the host and other family members, and then return home.

Around this time, Baai also felt an intense urge that I should have a family of my own. She even actively spoke to some of her acquaintances to enquire whether they knew a woman who could be suitable for me. She would also monitor my health closely and note even a slight loss of weight. She would then urge me to pay attention to my food intake and also take rest in order to prevent further weight loss.

Baai did not have much interest in watching television programmes. However, in 2015, I purchased and set up a television in her bedroom. The television set was positioned in such a way that she could see the screen even lying on her bed. She would practise self-restraint and usually watched only one daily-soap episode and a one-hour programme of songs. Occasionally, she watched the television in the company of a neighbour who would discuss the news with her.

As Baai could not climb down the staircase from her flat unassisted, she would not go out of house except on special occasions, such as visiting a relative's place for a function or going to the hospital for a medical check-up. She would often sit in a chair in the balcony of the flat and bask in the morning sun. Whenever I happened to be on the balcony with her, she would spot birds and identify them by their species.

When I would return home in the evening after work, Baai's face would light up. In case I was delayed in returning home, she would call me and enquire how much more time it would take for me to reach home. She continued to shower me with loving tenderness through her words, touch, smile, gaze, and several other actions, such as momentarily caressing my hair when I touched her feet to pay obeisance to her after my daily morning and evening prayers.

At the end of 2015, I purchased a flat on the ground floor of the same society where we lived, so that Baai could go out of the flat easily when required. However, later, upon close assessment, it was felt that the first-floor flat was better for various reasons such as ventilation, sunshine and a balcony. Hence, about four months after the ground floor flat was purchased, it was put on rent, as we continued to stay on the first floor.

∽

In late 2017, in the middle of the night, I heard Baai calling out to me, and when I reached her I found that she had had a fall. There was blood on her face, clotted. For quite a few years she had to pass urine a few times in the night, so she must have fallen while trying to visit the toilet on her own, not wanting to wake me for assistance since she knew I had to go to work early morning. Seeing her bleeding from the fall, I arranged for an ambulance and took her to the emergency unit of the hospital. The MRI scan revealed an internal brain injury and subdural haematoma, and hence she was shifted to an ICU of the hospital.

After four days, Baai was discharged from the hospital, as her condition seemed to be stable. Thereafter, her dullness and drowsiness increased and on the evening of Deepavali, she seemed to lose her alertness. An experienced physician examined her at home and advised that she be given intravenous saline. She resisted it, saying that she should now be freed and allowed to leave. Despite the intravenous saline administration to Baai that night, her condition did not improve in the morning and she seemed to have a lowered level of consciousness. Hence, she was again hospitalized in the morning and admitted to the ICU. Even after she was discharged from the hospital, her consciousness did not improve, nor did the swelling on her legs and arms.

After consulting a few other doctors, Baai was again hospitalized in a large hospital and was prepped for brain surgery. I went to a temple early morning on the day of her surgery, brought some prasaad from the temple, and placed a little in her mouth. My hectic work schedule during that period, together with the dismal prediction made by a neurosurgeon that Baai might go into a coma and die if the surgery was not immediately done, and her painful and worsening condition, prevented me from doing a more elaborate assessment of the likely benefits and risks of the brain surgery.

In the large hospital, the burr hole surgery was performed on Baai in order to remove some of the blood clotted inside her brain due to an internal brain injury. She was moved to a semi-intensive care unit. Over the next few days, her alertness improved, but then later she had a relapse, and her legs and arms began to swell again. Because of such a deterioration in her condition just a couple of days after the surgery, Baai had a feeder tube inserted through her nose to provide her water and liquid food, a tube to pass urine, a small tube in her brain to allow fluids to get discharged from the surgery hole, and an oxygen mask for breathing. Even in this state, a nurse attending to her told me that whenever she had an adequate level of consciousness at night, she could be heard chanting the holy name of God.

After a few days, she was moved out of the semi-intensive care unit to a separate room. In that room, when I asked her where we would go from there, Baai responded by saying that we would go to whichever place God had decided for us. She referred to the specific God in the form of Pandurang (a form of Lord Vishnu that is worshipped in the path of devotion). Thus, even in that state, Baai's union with God and faith in God remained.

As her condition deteriorated, the neurosurgeon decided, in response to my persistent requests that he should do everything possible for Baai's recovery, to perform a second burr hole surgery in order to remove blood clots formed inside her brain. As she had been in the hospital for about a month, my relatives suggested that I should consider resuming work from Monday. Her body was aided by several support systems for breathing, feeding and carrying bodily waste. Anyone in her situation would be filled with grief, frustration, anxiety and fear, but she was tranquil, the expressions on her face were serene, and she seemed to be devoid of grief, frustration or anxiety. Possibly, Baai's soul had attained union with the supreme soul and thus she had developed considerable disengagement from her body and its sufferings, and was in the serene state of pure consciousness.

Following the second brain surgery, she was kept in the ICU. On the day following her second surgery, when I entered the ICU during the visiting hours, even in her serious condition, she was uninterruptedly chanting God's divine name '*Raam, Raam, Raam, Raam...*' Her voice was clear and her words were unfaltering. Her face was clear, eyes wide open and with no fear in them. The effects of long-endured pain were not visible on her face.

I massaged Baai's legs and arms and asked her how it felt, and she responded by saying, 'It feels nice.' Then I gently kissed her on her forehead or cheek, and asked her how it was, to which she responded by saying that it was sweet ('*god aahe*'). As I left her at the end of the permitted visiting time of the ICU, I said 'bye' to her and she responded by saying the same. As I left, two of Baai's grandsons came to visit her, but she did not utter any word during their visit to her. Thus, her 'bye' to me was possibly her last word before leaving this world for her eternal divine abode.

A few minutes after I had come out of the ICU and while I was sitting in the waiting area praying for her recovery, the ICU staff called me into the unit and informed me that her heart had stopped functioning, even after attempts to resuscitate her. Looking back, I realized that Baai's last words and expressions at the moment of her leaving this world were of acceptance, contentment, serenity and concern for others, as she maintained her connection with God through chanting God's name. Her body was not functioning anymore, while her consciousness or soul was already detached from this world and united with the Supreme consciousness.

Baai had departed her severely impaired and tormented physical vessel, while retaining till her last moment of life a visage of clarity, a keen memory, and a mind steadfastly fixed on God. She was liberated. I realized this meaning of liberation from witnessing her final stages. In *Dnyaneshwari*, such a state of making a passage out of a physical body is described as the sign of a human being who has reached the highest form of spiritual development, termed '*brahma-bhava*', which implies the oneness of the mind with the supreme soul (the Brahman) or divine/pure consciousness[1]. Similar body-leaving processes were also reported for other individuals who pursued a spiritual life, such as

Shri Vinoba Ji Bhave. Such individuals could retain a serene state of awareness while leaving their bodily form toward the end of their stay in this world.

Attainment of this state is the phase indicating that one had already received God's grace, union with God, liberation from the physical body, and a culmination of the lifelong pursuit of the divine through various paths. This is the state possibly reflected in Gandhiji's non-violent response while bullets were pumped into his body and his body was approaching its death. During the last few days in the life of Shri Vinoba Ji Bhave, his deteriorating body's physiological functioning parameters kept causing worries to doctors attending to him, but he himself remained in a serene state while at times chanting or silently murmuring God's divine name[2]. This state is somewhat similar to that of Sant Shri Dnyaneshwar Ji Maharaj who decided to deliberately separate his consciousness from his physical body. He did this possibly because his consciousness had already attained a union with the Supreme consciousness, hence its removal from the body while the body would gradually disintegrate, and its merger with the Supreme consciousness was attained through the process of samadhi. Thus, Baai had attained the last stage that was somewhat similar to the state of union with the divine that various spiritual aspirants and holy saints had attained or expressed at the time of their leaving this world.

GLEANINGS

- Baai had, through various phases of her life and during the serious adversities in her life, maintained remembrance of God, even in the most painful moment of leaving her physical body. A person who leaves the physical body while maintaining remembrance of God, attains oneness with God[3]. Therefore, it is advised that one should continually maintain remembrance of God.[4]
- Such a state of liberation from the physical body was reflected in the absence of fear, anxiety and frustration in her, and the presence of serenity, even when her body was in a tormented and frail state. She exhibited how one could, by living an ordinary life, attain union with God, self-realization, and liberation from the physical self.

PART II

BAAI'S LIFE: A LESSON IN SPIRITUAL STRENGTH

6
Baai: An Embodiment of Noble Virtues

Even though she lived in great hardship in many phases of her life, Baai was content and thankful to God for helping her deal virtuously with her impoverished circumstances and enabling her to fulfil her duties to those around her. Among her virtues, Baai prized honesty and industriousness. She would never accept money or any commodity from anyone without having earned it. She used to honestly earn her wages by doing what was required. In fact, she was so conscientious with her work that even stringent farm supervisors found it unnecessary to monitor Baai's work as a farm labourer. Even though she would sometimes arrive late at the farm, they knew she would compensate for her late arrival with her hard work. In another instance, despite her impoverished state, she resisted the temptation to dilute the milk she sold. Baai's adherence to honesty remained strict and unconditional.

Baai's house and kitchen used to be spotless. Clothes would get heavily soiled as dust was everywhere on the village roads. Modern detergent powders for washing clothes were unavailable, and there was no access to free-flowing tap water. Instead, water was stored in containers. She fetched water from the container again and again, and used to exert immense physical strength to ensure the cleanliness of her family members' clothes.

Baai maintained internal purity and always had innocent intentions and thoughts. She never harboured malicious intent to deceive anyone or derive benefits from others, and she always upheld truthfulness. On one occasion, Baai's husband was threatened by the village's influential persons to make an untruthful statement on an important matter. Despite considerable pressure on them, Baai advised Bhaau, who himself had a strong commitment to truthfulness, that he should not make an untruthful statement irrespective of the demands by the powerful people. Later, they had to pay for their honesty by suffering some adverse consequences.

Baai's industriousness was extraordinary. She used to be engaged in various strenuous work from the wee hours of the morning till the late hours of the night, and used to get only a few hours of sleep. She also expressed determination and courage. For example, even in the face of a few years of ill health and the loss of Bhaau's earnings, and of agricultural land and cattle, Baai determinedly worked hard to fulfil her duties and garnered the courage to face adversities by praying for strength and support.

Baai lived by the value of non-violence. She never nursed the intent to cause emotional or physical harm to anyone, including those who had wronged her. In fact, she used to say that there is the soul or the divine (aatma) in every creature, and that one should not harbour resentment towards anyone. Instead, one should try to bring as much happiness to others as possible. She used to say that we should empathize with others ('*dusaryacha jeeva jaanaava*') and would also say that one's words, gestures and smile should be such that it reduces everyone's distress, and provides happiness to all.

In one incident, a part of her cattle-shed area was taken forcibly by her neighbour, who was intending to house his cattle there. He was a socially influential person and was inclined to engage in violence. In this incident, Baai chose to accept the loss of some areas of the cattle-shed to avoid provoking violence. Kindness, compassion and altruism were also among the divine virtues that Baai practised.

∽

While working in the kitchen of a large hostel catering to about 100 students, not only did she cook for them but also served them with love and devotion. She knew they were away from their parents, and felt it necessary to provide them with affection and good food.

The students adored Baai. Despite the inadequate ingredients in the hostel kitchen for making curries, she compensated by putting in extra effort and care to ensure the curries were delicious. Consequently, while curries prepared by other ladies were occasionally discarded, Baai's were always relished by the students. Whenever she made curries, the students would eat more pieces of bhaakari. She used to feel great satisfaction seeing the students eating heartily despite being away from their homes. She treated them like her own children. On the festival day of Dasara, the students would visit Baai's home to pay her obeisance and she would welcome them with affection.

Baai exuded compassion in many ways. Once, a little boy from a poor family fell ill, but his parents could not stay with him, as they were compelled to go to distant farm fields to work as casual labourers. The little boy's house was about 100 m away from Baai's, and whenever possible he used to come and sit in her house. In his weakened condition, he would lean against a wall in her home. Baai gave him both emotional nourishment and food. This continued for several days until the boy recovered. She never took credit for her good deeds. Instead, she saw it as fulfilling her duty. She possibly saw God's manifestation in the diseased, hungry and helpless little boy. Similarly, a little girl, from a house close to Baai's, used to come and sit at her home. That little girl also used to receive food, care and affection from Baai, and she would often resist leaving Baai's home even when others would tell her to return to her own.

∽

Baai knew of an unconventional remedy for a scorpion bite. In the villages, scorpions would appear in several places: under stones in empty plots and also in houses. Hence, people would often become victims of sudden scorpion bites. She administered the remedy for those who sought help without charging any money, although the ingredients of the remedy accrued some cost. She would even tend to the victims at odd hours, such as late at night or even when she was having her dinner.

In her village, a poor family did not have their land and had to rely on the earnings they received from hard labour. The woman in that family became ill and hence could not breastfeed her newborn child. The child was also sickly. Baai breastfed that child and the child survived. In another case, a poor lady would often face the situation of not having enough flour in her house to make meals and feed her family. She would come to Baai's home and quietly stand at a spot where Baai could see her, but she would not ask for flour out of embarrassment. Baai understood the situation, and, despite her poverty, she would give some flour to the poor lady, often concealing this from her in-laws.

In the village, some women were suffering because of harsh treatment by their husbands. They used to be in grief and anguish, and could not share their problems with anyone. Their maternal homes used to be quite some distance away, and the modern modes of distant communication (such as telephones) were not readily available in those days in rural areas. Sensing Baai's compassion and selfless service, they would often confide in her. They would talk to her when they were working together, such as when fetching water from the well, or while doing casual labourers' work, such as grass weeding. Baai used to listen patiently and with empathy, advising them to display patience, endurance and forgiveness. She also used to guide them on ways to develop inner strength to withstand adversities.

The modes of transport between villages were bullock carts and buses (owned by government transport corporations). One such bus from a district town used to come to Baai's village late at night. This was the last stop. From here, those who stayed in villages a few miles away would walk on a difficult, unlit trail filled with pebbles and potholes. Hence, walking the distance between two villages at night used to be risky. Baai and Bhaau used to provide such travellers with water, serve them dinner, and provide them shelter to sleep for the night. The following day, these people used to leave Baai's home and walk toward their villages.

In those days, pilgrims would go on foot from their villages to holy places of pilgrimage like Alandi, Paithan or Pandharpur. They would walk far toward their destination during the day, chanting God's holy name and singing abhangas. These pilgrims were called *vaarkari*s (from the word *vaari*, meaning 'a trip to the place of pilgrimage'). After walking through the day, they would halt overnight in a village on their way. They would usually stay in some temple. Some would have their family members, such as wives and children, with them. In Baai's village, such vaarkaris usually stayed in the temple of Lord Hanuman. After his day's tailoring work, Bhaau would visit the Hanuman temple in the evening to pay his obeisance. Upon seeing vaarkaris there, he would ask them from where they had come, where they were planning to go the next day, and whether they had any arrangements for dinner. If not, he would invite them home.

Baai would then get busy in preparing extra quantities of dinner. After they had had their dinner, the pilgrims would return to the temple for sleep. Thereafter, Baai and Bhaau would have their dinner. Though exhausted from the day's work, she willingly cooked dinner for the pilgrims without any complaint or hesitation. Instead, she did this additional work with zeal, in the form of service and devotion to God. She used to say that she felt immense satisfaction seeing others happy and fulfilled (*'itarancha jeeva/aatma trupta hotana paahun svatahalaa sukh vaatane'*).

∽

Baai also practised the noble values of simplicity, austerity and endurance. An example of this comes from the following incident. Baai had once visited her married daughter who lived in a distant city around 200 km away. Upon reaching the city, she walked from the bus station to her daughter's place without taking any mode of transport. Being new to the city, she reached her daughter's house by asking directions from strangers. After spending a few days at her daughter's home, Baai planned to return to her village. The first bus she took went only till a town, quite some distance from her village. She got down there at night and had to wait till morning for the second bus. She had neither money to stay in a paid shelter like a lodge, nor any relatives or acquaintances there. At that point, it occurred to her that a family from her village had a cycle shop in that town. Feeling it might be more appropriate to seek shelter in the cycle shop rather than remain at the bus station, she requested the cycle shop owner to let her sleep in the shop's front yard for the night. She kept her luggage bag, stitched of cloth, under her head and slept on the floor in front of the cycle shop. In the morning, without having tea or breakfast, she walked back to the bus station and boarded the bus for her village, reaching there in a few hours. It is also unlikely that she had dinner that night. Upon returning home, she discovered a large volume of work that had piled up due to her absence. She dived straight into her strenuous work routine, without paying attention to her fatigue and hunger. Such was her acceptance and endurance of life's hardships.

Here is another example of Baai's sense of acceptance and courage to face adversities. Accompanied by her mother-in-law, she was once returning from some work in the field when heavy rain started. Under the heavy torrents of water, the cracks in the ground began to widen and fill with rainwater. It was likely that snakes would emerge from those cracks, and so Baai and her mother-in-law took shelter in a cattle-shed, where they spent a considerable part of the night drenched. Baai remained unperturbed, possibly softly murmuring God's holy name until the rain subsided.

∽

Baai's in-laws had dealt with her harshly early on, permitting only inadequate hours of sleep and amount of food, and making her toil all day. Yet, Baai had a forgiving nature. When her father-in-law, who used to be called 'Daada', became old, he was sick and frail. Baai took great care of him, giving him warm water for a bath and applying coconut oil to the wounds on his body. She would also prepare tea and hold the saucer close to his lips so that he could sip the warm tea from it. Tears used to roll down Daada's eyes whenever he expressed his repentance for having treated Baai harshly in her childhood. In such instances, she would console and urge him not to remember the past. He also told her that she reminded him of his mother, possibly because of the care that she took of him. Baai's service to Daada reflected her complete and unconditional forgiveness, a sense of duty, and an awareness that there is a divine soul in every living being.

A touching expression of Baai's forgiveness and compassion was when she was hospitalized at the age of about 90 in 2013. At that time, she suffered from several ailments, including pneumonia, heart attack, stroke and skeletal tuberculosis. Her body had immense swelling, it was difficult for her to speak, and she occasionally lost consciousness. Some of Baai's relatives used to visit her in the hospital. One was a person from whose near ones

Baai had suffered some neglect. When Baai became aware of that person next to her bed, she wanted to place her palms on his head to bless him but could not, as her hands were swollen and too heavy to lift. So, she asked her son to lift her hand and place it on that person's head. Baai had wholeheartedly forgiven that person for his association with those from whom she had suffered some neglect.

GLEANINGS

The divine values expressed through Baai's actions include industriousness, simplicity, frugality, austerity, endurance, courage, determination, external and internal cleanliness, guilelessness, honesty, truthfulness, abstinence from greed and envy, contentment, a sense of duty, forgiveness, non-violence, kindness, compassion, charity, and focusing on service to others as a form of worship and devotion to God. In doing such selfless service, she naturally underwent *sadhana* (self-purifying living or conduct) or *tapasyaa* (prolonged regimented practice, spiritual austerities, or penances) as a means of attaining union with God through work (karma yoga) and through devotion (bhakti yoga) in particular. From her virtues and life of service, we can learn how to:

- not harm others
- empathize with all
- work towards alleviating the sorrows of others, even amid one's struggles
- view the divine presence in all beings
- practise ethical conduct through adherence to virtues such as truthfulness, honesty and guilelessness

- practise virtues such as endurance, patience, industriousness and forgiveness

Adopting such values and engaging in selfless service dedicated to God are means of treading on the path of self-transcendence. Such a way of living can facilitate a connection with God through karma yoga and bhakti yoga. *Dnyaneshwari* suggests that virtuous deeds purify the mind[1], doing one's God-ordained work is the supreme service to God[2] and a way of realizing God[3], viewing God in every being is itself bhakti yoga[4], and rendering altruistic service to others is a way of becoming God's devotee[5].

7

Facing Hardships by Oneself, While Serving Others

Despite going through several hardships, Baai did not develop any sense of bitterness towards life. Instead, she practised acceptance and perseverance while dealing with hardships, upheld high ethical standards, and maintained devotion to God. As mentioned previously, Baai's mother, Lahaani Aai, used to provide joy to her family by cooking inexpensive yet special, delicious food on festive days. Baai had probably acquired the mindset to be content with life and provide others the little joys of it from her mother.

Deepavali celebrations had great religious, familial and social significance in rural areas during those days. In this festival, Goddess Lakshmi (the goddess of wealth) was worshipped for adequate wealth. This festival also symbolized the eradication of evil and the celebration of Goddess Lakshmi's victory over the demon Narakaasur. On this occasion, family members elaborately prepared and enjoyed delicacies together. Houses were repaired, cleaned and painted a couple of days before the festival, while new clothes used to be bought for all. Children would burst crackers, and houses would become illuminated with several diyas. Family members would anoint their bodies with scented paste, bathe with fragrant soaps, wear new clothes, and feast on the delicacies specially prepared for Deepavali. This festival had a lot of social significance, as families would invite their acquaintances and exchange platefuls of sweets.

Baai's approach to life, of acceptance and providing joy to others, was reflected in her preparations for and celebration of Deepavali. Her preparations would start several days before the festival of lights. First, the clay walls of the house were repaired and plastered. The house would decay over the year, with cracks developing on the wall's surface and small patches of the wall's coating peeling off. The walls were patched up by plastering them with clay slurry. For this, clay had to be dug up and then sieved. Then, a thick paste would be made of this and pasted on the entire wall.

After the plastering and maintenance work, which would go on for days, she would prepare special delicacies for family members to eat. At times, this work commenced during the period of the plastering, which meant that Baai would work on the plastering during the day and on the food delicacies at night.

On the day of Deepavali, Baai would get up early. Sometimes, she would not sleep the night before due to the constant preparations. She would prepare hot bath water for the children at the break of dawn, rub perfumed bathing-paste on them, and then give them a nice bath. Then, she would dress them with new clothes and offer them platefuls of delicacies prepared by her. She would feed them the festive meals with great love. In the evening, she would place several earthen and wick-lit lamps around the house and give the children some crackers to burst. Baai would be so engaged during this period that she often did not get to eat the delicacies she prepared. Her greatest happiness was in giving care, joy and happiness to others.

∽

Baai displayed a sense of duty, determination, courage and perseverance in the face of overwhelming adversities. She must have been around 40 when she faced a series of adversities. As mentioned earlier, Bhaau became seriously ill due to which he had to stop his tailoring work. Thus, the burden of providing for the family fell on Baai. Around the same time, there was shortage of rain for the crops for a few consecutive years, so agricultural activities were significantly reduced and food shortages emerged. In fact, the income from Baai's small piece of agricultural land simply stopped. As there was no fodder to feed the cattle, the cattle was unable to produce a good quantity of milk. During that period, the available option was the government-funded work of digging a quarry outside the village and breaking large stones from the quarry excavation into small ones, which were then sold to the construction industry as raw material. Baai had no choice but to take up the arduous work of breaking stones at the quarry.

In the quarry, after a series of explosions, large and small pieces of stone would loosen from the quarry ground and fly in the air. Labourers would rush to collect thin stone pieces because breaking them into small pieces required less effort. The stones had to be pounded with a hammer to break them into small chips. This work was strenuous and fatiguing, as it was conducted in the scorching heat of the sun. Depending on the volume of stone chips produced, one used to receive the payment.

Once, while Baai was holding a large stone with one hand and pounding it with a hammer, she accidentally injured her finger. Over the next few days, the wound on her finger festered and she could not fall asleep all night. The wound could not heal for some time, as she had to continue with household chores and hammering stones at the quarry during the day. She persevered with courage and determination, and did not allow her situation to overwhelm her in any way.

Her strenuous work schedule continued with limited sleep. Lack of nutritious food resulted in Baai becoming weak and anaemic. However, she drew strength from her awareness that her responsibilities were unavoidable, from her faith in God, and from her prayers to the Almighty.

∽

Baai also followed high ethical standards and had a strong sense of justice. Once, when she was employed as a cook in the kitchen of a hostel mess, the supervisor accused a woman labourer of misappropriating grocery items from the kitchen. Baai protested to the supervisor on behalf of the labourer and thereafter quit her job, even while knowing that quitting would require her to go to distant fields for work. Yet, she was prepared to do so rather than compromise on the principles of justice and integrity.

She continued upholding high ethical standards with constant engagement in devotional worship of God. Amidst the drudgery of her chores, she continually engaged in *chintan* (contemplation) while silently repeating God's divine name. For example, as part of her job in the hostel kitchen, she made the powder of the ingredients of spices daily using a mortar and pestle (*khal batta*). This work was strenuous, as it required pounding the ingredients placed in the mortar with a heavy metal pestle. With every pounding stroke, Baai used to silently utter God's divine name. She also observed fasts as a mode of expressing devotion to God and occasionally went on pilgrimages.

While engaged in her daily chores, Baai sometimes sang abhangas. Though exhausted at the end of her day, she used to thank God for helping her meet the requirements of that day. In serving and helping others in several ways, Baai was aware that all are manifestations of God and that God's element or essence (jeeva) is present in each.

∽

She developed several homespun ways to help her cope with impoverished circumstances. For example, she would wrap an old cloth around her children's shoulders to protect them from the cold winters. During monsoons, she would put a folded gunny bag on her children's heads to protect them from the rain. During certain parts of the crop cultivation cycle, work such as uprooting the standing crop plants had to be done throughout the day. On such occasions, to start work in the distant agriculture field at the break of day and avoid the travel time between home and the field, she would temporarily live there for a few days. As the open fields used to get cold at night, she would make a shallow spot in the ground by raking up the soil to protect herself from cold. The shallow spot in the ground provided a little warmth as she slept.

In those days, life was particularly arduous for women, as they had to cook food in earthen and metal pots on a chullah. The intensity of the fire had to be reduced by varying the quantity of wood in the fire or moving the burning sticks back and forth. At night, the chullah had to be cleaned by mopping it with a slurry made from soil and water. Then, in the morning, a little kerosene would be poured onto a few wooden planks or sticks, and they would be lit with a matchstick after being placed in the chullah. To spread the fire from a few wooden planks and sticks to all, one would blow air towards the fuelwood using a metal blowpipe. All of this was time-consuming. This work had to be done in the dim light of a wick lamp, as electricity became available only when Baai was about 40–45. Her cooking was simple. It did not have much oil or abundant cooking ingredients such as spices, groundnuts and coconuts. Yet, her food was delicious. Possibly, the key to her tasty food was not only the care she put into cooking but also that she remembered God while cooking.

In those days, detergent for washing clothes was also not readily available. To wash clothes, Baai had to take them to a distant place outside the village where a quarry was located. The quarry used to be filled with water seeping from its walls. This water was unfit for drinking and hence could be used only for washing clothes. Clothes used to get heavily soiled and stained because roads were not covered with either tar or cement. Before washing, the clothes had to be boiled in water mixed with washing soda to loosen the dirt. Then, the clothes had to be thumped and beaten hard on stones to get the dirt out. Finally, the clothes would be rinsed and washed in water, squeezed to rid them of the extra water, and then hung on a line for drying.

The daily work of obtaining water for drinking and other household activities was also strenuous, as there was no tap water. Each family would regularly go to one specific well, and possibly to the well closest to the family's house. One had to carry a couple of pitchers and a small but heavy metal bucket with a long, thick rope tied to its handle. Once the bucket had wholly sunk into the well and was filled with the well water, one had to pull it out by pulling the rope upwards. At times, as Baai used to be engaged in several activities during the day, the water-fetching work could be done only during the night. She would walk to the distant well, draw water from it, and carry large water-filled pitchers back home on her head.

> ### GLEANINGS
>
> While engaged in her daily chores, Baai would sing abhangas and be continually involved in chintan. No matter what difficulties were thrust upon her, she dealt with them through acceptance, industriousness, courage, remembering God, and having unswerving faith in God. One can learn several things from her devotion, such as:
>
> - seeing others as a manifestation of God and offering service to them as a service to God
> - providing joy to others while serving them
> - remembering God in one's daily life, while one is working
> - trying not to compromise on ethics and justice
> - dealing with adversities through acceptance, industriousness, courage and faith in God—this itself is a form of service to God, reflecting the acceptance of God-ordained circumstances, commitment to God-ordained duties, and acknowledgement of God's presence in all

8

Baai's Approach to the Adversities of Life

Baai's qualities and values set her apart from others, including her high endurance level, patience and compassion. Baai had immense faith in God. These qualities and values gave her peace and led her to spiritual development. One abhanga of Sant Shri Tukaram Ji Maharaj[1] indicates that one can attain peace by keeping one's mind free from negative thoughts such as envy, keeping one's mind clear, and practising forgiveness.

Baai used to say that she tried not to let bad thoughts fester. Like a sieve, one must only retain the useful grains and eliminate the waste, or like a slate, our mind should be repeatedly cleaned. Another metaphor she used was of a river, which leaves dirt at the bottom and continues to flow with clean water. Similarly, she said that one should leave behind one's negative experiences and be in the present, while focusing on the future with a clean mind. She advised others to follow a similar approach to deal with their problems. Baai would not complain about things that would cause her inconvenience, as she did not want others to feel unhappy.

She preferred to accept hardships rather than complain about them. Even in her old age and ill health, she tried to be as self-reliant as possible. In her old age, she made conscious attempts to remain active and would say that if she stopped moving her limbs, her activity level and alertness would decrease. She also maintained her cheerfulness, and concern and compassion for others.

Living alone in old age must have been challenging. However, when I, Baai's youngest son, told her that I felt sad about not being able to live with her due to my distant job location, Baai said that she did not feel lonely, as she had God with her. She added that God protected her in this final phase of her life. Baai's faith in God was a source of support for her in many ways.

∽

Baai's concern and affection for her children were apparent even as she aged and suffered ill health. She would, at times, ask her children not to visit her so frequently so that their work and their families were not affected. When talking to them on the telephone or in person, Baai would say that she was well and was resting even if she was ill and in pain. She would enquire about their well-being and urge them to pay attention to proper eating and rest. Her unconditional acceptance, love and care as a mother were visible till the end. Such readiness to accept suffering for oneself while aiming to avoid any inconvenience to others, and maintaining concern for the well-being of others, are said to be the qualities of a saint, according to one abhanga by Sant Shri Tukaram Ji Maharaj.[2] Her only regret seemed to be how hard she had worked for the betterment of some people who had neglected her. However, on this aspect also, she would return to a serene state of mind, saying that she had offered all her deeds to God and she had forgiven all.

To convey the importance of forgiveness and service, she said that a river allows its water to quench the thirst not only of a cow but also of a wild beast. Similarly, her compassion did not discriminate between people. The importance of such an orientation in attaining oneness with God is reflected in an abhanga of Sant Shri Tukaram Ji Maharaj.[3]

Baai's interest in and concern for others was remarkable. Even when she was hospitalized and suffered spells of unconsciousness, she enquired about the family circumstances of the ICU's woman security guard, as Baai had developed an affection for her. She never expressed anger because of others' vices or behaviour, as she maintained a constant awareness that God exists in every human being. She also deeply understood feelings, thereby comprehending the reasons for others' misbehaviour. In this way, her mind remained serene and Baai could forgive others and be at peace. She would say that had she not kept aside the anguish and pain caused by others, she would have collapsed under the burden of life's adversities.

Baai not only dealt with adversities in her life but also helped others. The value of such an orientation in nurturing devotion to God is reflected in an abhanga of Sant Shri Tukaram Ji Maharaj.[4] Several drastic changes in her circumstances took place at different periods. She took these changes in her stride and adapted harmoniously.

∽

When Baai was a child, her father passed away. This led to several hardships, including tattered clothes, a meagre livelihood, loss of her father's affection, and demanding work at a tender age. She displayed a sense of acceptance and persevered through difficult times with hard work and being constantly engaged in religious activities. An early marriage and a loveless life, due to punitive in-laws who treated her harshly, added to her woes. Yet, she never blamed her mother for marrying her off to a harsh family, never resisted her in-laws' diktats, and did not complain to anyone. Instead, she prayed to God to provide her endurance to bear the harsh circumstances.

After only a few years of living with her in-laws, when she was about 10 or 12, her father-in-law took her to Paithan. He then located some known pilgrims and sat with them for a meal on the nearby riverbank. Baai also sat with him to partake in the meal. When she finished her meal and looked around, she discovered that her father-in-law had vanished. She was traumatized by this abandonment, especially as she had no idea how to return home. Luckily, some people who knew Lahaani Aai recognized Baai, and took her home. Neither Baai nor Lahaani Aai had any choice but to suffer this abandonment in silence.

It was not until a few years later that Baai's in-laws permitted her to come back. She did not hold any grudge against her in-laws and did not remind them of their past ill-treatment. Instead, she politely returned to her in-laws only to resume her strenuous work and to face continued ill-treatment.

∽

As part of the strenuous efforts to support the family of eight and to obtain some economic security, Baai and

Bhaau would accept agricultural land from other families for cultivation, for which they would receive a share of the farm produce. The family's frugal living eventually resulted in some savings, enabling Baai and Bhaau to purchase a small portion of agricultural land.

Baai ensured that her children got access to education and regularly attended schools rather than working as child labourers. She made considerable efforts to support her children's education, from cleaning and ironing their school uniforms to making them meals on time. She never asked her children to do any housework that could interfere with their education. In those days, education in the village was only up to the high-school level. Sending one's child to study beyond high school at distant places was difficult because of the economic burden. Hence, few families sent their children outside to study. Baai's progressive outlook and determination to provide a promising future for her children resulted in her sending her eldest child to a distant town for higher education. The financial burden entailed further hardships and sacrifices. For example, she had to deprive her children of drinking the cow's milk at home so that she could sell it to pay for a part of her eldest son's higher education and living expenses.

Her schedule was so hectic that while performing one task she used to plan the next one awaiting her attention. She would walk briskly, and her nimble hands moved at great speed. Often sleep-deprived, she would get up early in the morning and quickly rush through her chores. This hectic daily routine was so ingrained in her that when she was around 90, she would still wake up in the morning and try and rush to do some work, only to realize that her legs had become weak with age, meaning that she could not even walk without the support of a walking stick.

Due to economic hardships, at times Baai would wear a sari made from stitching together two old saris. Sometimes, the two old saris would be of different colours, which made her poverty highly visible. Yet, she was not embarrassed by it. She firmly believed that people should not be ashamed of their impoverished situation or of doing laborious or menial work.

∽

While carrying out the daily routine of strenuous activities, she also, selflessly and altruistically, contributed to society. A community feast used to be arranged on occasions such as weddings or family functions. On such occasions, some families would invite her to cook dishes that required special culinary skills, such as curries or sweet *halwa* (*sheera*). Baai would accept such invitations and return home without taking any payment or food items that she cooked. In this way, she would help the community through altruistic service.

There were times in her life when she underwent immense suffering. At one point, her legs swelled due to the advanced stage of pregnancy and inadequate nourishment leading to weakness during that time, and the strenuous nature of work in the field. Furthermore, field work led to small wounds from the sharp chips (*dhaskat*) of crops piercing into her palms. Her body became so weak that a doctor admonished her family members, saying that there was danger to her life. However, her faith in God remained steadfast even in those dire circumstances. During her severe adversities, she prayed for God's support and thanked God for seeing her through the day. In her life, there existed a delicate balance between determination and acceptance, courage and humility, industriousness and faith, aspirations for a brighter future and contentment with the present, adherence to stringent personal ethics and forgiveness for others' ethical lapses, and honest, ethically sound efforts to overcome poverty without harbouring envy towards others' prosperity. Simultaneously, she maintained the chintan of God, chanted God's name, and engaged in explicit religious activities such as listening to religious scriptures and spiritual discourses when feasible.

To sum up, during the initial stage of Baai's life, her early childhood was marked by the absence of a family-owned home, landlessness, and her upbringing in poverty without the protective care of a father. The second part of her early childhood went into suffering harsh treatment, including doing strenuous work and being sleep-deprived at her in-laws'. The third part of her early childhood went in being abandoned by her in-laws and getting sent to her mother's home. The adolescent and adult years of Baai's life went into a hectic routine of strenuous activities and laborious work to move out of poverty and pave a progressive path for her children through access to education. She continuously had faith in God, and strict adherence to ethical conduct and virtues in all these phases. Her work and life became a way of forming a union with God.

GLEANINGS

- Some of Baai's qualities and values reflect those of a devotee[5] (*bhakta*), a person with self-knowledge[6] (*dnyaan*), and a person with a divine (*daivee*)[7] disposition as opposed to a demonic (*aasuri*) disposition. Such qualities of a devotee make one dear (*priya*) to God[8] and can be instrumental in one's liberation (*moksha*)[9].
- She reflected values associated with individual spirituality[10], and with ethical and spiritual well-being[11].

PART III

DRAWING TOGETHER THE SPIRITUAL ELEMENTS IN BAAI'S LIFE

9

A View Based on the Scientific Literature on Spirituality

While the preceding chapters focused on Baai's life and her general spiritual outlook, this chapter first describes the scientific literature on spirituality and outlines some features of spiritual development. The latter part of this chapter links these features of spiritual development with Baai's life to illustrate the manifestation of complex and abstract spiritual ideas in the life of an ordinary mother like her.

∽

Although spirituality has been studied extensively, it is striking to note that there is no universally accepted definition of the same. In fact, there are about 40 definitions of spirituality.[1] Furthermore, the scientific literature does not have an established position as to whether spirituality and religion are the same phenomenon. While some view them as the same, others regard spirituality and religion as different.[2]

One similarity is that spirituality and religion focus on the sacred.[3] Consistent with this, L. Seidlitz and others have reported that a panel of leading researchers and scholars identified the sacred and its search as the main element in spirituality and religion.[4] Another common element is selfless love.[5]

However, religion and spirituality also differ in various ways. One distinction is that religion focuses on the social, institutional or community-based shaping of an individual's experience of the transcendent, while spirituality focuses on an individual's relationship with transcendent phenomena such as God or the universe.[6] Consistent with this, it is observed that while spirituality and religion have the common element of the sacred, they differ in that the goals of a religion may also include non-sacred goals, such as welfare, and a religion has an associated social group.[7] Further, it is indicated that religion seeks the sacred in the form of the divine, while spirituality seeks the sacred as larger sacredness.[8] In other words, spirituality may seek sacredness in forms other than the divine—such as idealism, meaning, purpose and connectedness with other human beings—though the divine may also be included as the sacred in spirituality.

P.C. Hill and K.I. Pargament, though, have provided reasons why it may not be appropriate to separate religion and spirituality.[9] They noted that the concepts of spirituality and religion are interrelated[10] and can be seen as overlapping.[11]

In the following discussion, the focus is mainly on spirituality. In the scientific literature on spirituality, the terms 'sacred' and 'transcendent' are frequently used as the ultimate objective of spiritual pursuits or as the aim of spirituality. For example, Hill and Pargament, in defining spirituality, note that spirituality can be viewed as the process by which individuals explore, find, retain, and even change if needed, something that in their life has the status of the sacred.[12] Others view spirituality as the transcendence need[13] or potential for transcendence.[14] These views suggest that seeking the transcendent and the sacred are key features of spirituality, and each of these two are described below.

∽

The term 'transcendence' refers to climbing over[15], stepping beyond the boundaries of the location and period of the self[16], and going beyond[17]. This suggests that transcendence is going beyond the apparent or the physical appearance to comprehend more significant principles and forces, or more fundamental truths and reality.

Further, L.W. Fry notes that the notion of 'calling' involves benefitting others through one's service and deriving a sense of transcendence.[18] R.L. Piedmont mentions that transcendence can also be expressed through a self-sacrificing orientation to benefit others.[19] This may suggest that transcendence is also attained by going beyond one's self-interests. Further, C.W. Ellison notes that transcendence refers to the ability to find a sense of purpose from something that is not centred on one's self and also from having a relationship with God.[20]

Thus, transcendence of one's immediate aspects such as the concern for the physical self and material interests, serving others, and connecting with God are different facets of transcendence. Both these aspects of going beyond self-interests and connecting to God seem to have a common aspect of transcending the self. Consistent with this, Hill and Pargament note that spirituality involves going beyond oneself to link oneself to a larger positive aspect such as the pursuit of meaning and purpose, and placing one's identity within a tradition, a thought system, or a collective.[21] This suggests that transcendence involves going beyond self-interests or serving an ideal, or is linked to a collective while functioning in the world and/or connecting to God or the divine. The various forms of transcendence are reflected in Ellison's work, which notes that all items in the spiritual well-being scale focus on transcendent matters such as the experience associated with meaning, purpose, positive ideals, and a sense of connection with God.[22]

Thus, the literature suggests that transcendence can be attained in two forms. Firstly, it can be attained by transcending the self through having self-transcending purposes and meaning in the world. Secondly, transcendence can be attained by transcending the self through connecting with God. While elaborating on spiritual well-being, Ellison uses the terms 'horizontal' and 'vertical' dimensions to refer to the existential and religious (or God-related) aspects of spiritual well-being.[23] Drawing on this terminology, attainment of transcendence through self-interest transcending means (such as having a meaning and purpose) and attainment of transcendence through a connection with God can be viewed respectively as horizontal and vertical dimensions of self-transcendence.

That the horizontal dimension of transcendence implies going beyond self-interests is reflected in Piedmont's view, which suggests that subordinating one's benefit for the benefits of others through behaviours such as altruism reflects transcendence.[24] Further, as mentioned previously, Fry notes that the notion of 'calling' implies an experience of transcendence and an experience of meaning and purpose from rendering other-benefitting services.[25] This implies that transcendence involves going beyond one's self-interest for doing good to others through self-sacrificing altruism. The vertical dimension of transcendence involves connecting to God, the divine, the ultimate truth, and such phenomena.

∽

In understanding the related term 'sacred' that, in the scientific literature on spirituality, serves as the destination or objective of spirituality, it may be noted that the term 'sacred' denotes those aspects that are worthy of adoration or worship and include the notions of the ultimate reality, conceptions of divine, the construct of God, and the transcendent aspects as well as other phenomena in life derived from or linked to these aspects, as Hill and Pargament describe.[26] This suggests that the terms 'sacred' and 'transcendent' have the same meaning and refer to something beyond the ordinary and worthy of veneration. Further, many scholars refer to spiritual transcendence as an experience of the sacred.[27] Thus, the several forms of transcendence mentioned earlier can also be viewed as forms of the sacred.

These various descriptions suggest that the terms 'sacred' and 'transcendent' both have similar meanings and refer to something an individual considers to be beyond his immediate time and space, beyond his material or physical self, beyond material self-interests—something that is important, venerable and reflective of the ultimate truth or ultimate reality. The sacred and transcendent can take on various forms such as a calling, a higher purpose, a meaning, the universe, an ideal, faith, the divine, the higher self, the inner self, the ultimate truth, the ultimate reality and God. Connecting with and experiencing the sacred and the transcendent implies a state of transcendence and the attainment of spirituality.[28] Thus, searching and striving for transcendence can be viewed as the process of spiritual development.

∽

Just as human beings have other needs, such as relating to others, they also have a need for transcendence.[29] This need for transcendence is referred to as the spiritual need.[30] P.L. Benson, E.C. Roehlkepartain and S.P. Rude refer to spirituality as the potential for transcending one's self to form a connection with something transcendent, and suggest that transcendence can be attained through various means such as having meaning and purpose, connecting to the sacred, and associating with a collective or a thought system.[31]

Similarly, Piedmont suggests that being altruistic and being loyal to a nation can be some ways in which transcendence can be expressed, and suggests that such expressions imply subordinating one's needs to larger groups.[32] Piedmont also suggests that spiritual transcendence involves appreciating the limited nature of one's perspective formed by one's immediate context, and having a way of understanding life that gives coherence and integration to all elements of existence, and addresses the core human cravings.[33]

Thus, Piedmont notes that transcendence, in a spiritual sense, is the potential for stepping beyond one's limited context to have a broader (rather than a subjective) view of life as it is.[34] This suggests that transcendence involves going beyond a self-centred perspective to understand life, and to see life from a perspective that provides coherence to the entire existence. This suggests that transcendence involves going beyond a fragmentary or narrow self-focused perspective to a broad, inclusive or unitive perspective of the universe or all existence. Thus, awareness of being in harmony with the universe or all existence also emerges as an expression of spirituality.

Ellison's expression suggests that the spiritual aspect refers to an aspect beyond the physical one.[35] The scientific literature also suggests that the spiritual dimension refers to an aspect that is beyond the material aspect.[36] These views from the literature on spirituality suggest that the spiritual dimension of human beings refers to the non-physical or non-material aspect of human existence. These views also suggest that spirituality involves going beyond one's self and being aware of one's connectedness with others.

The scientific literature also provides another view of spirituality as a connection with the higher consciousness or the transcendent. For example, one view suggests that spiritual development is the positive change that occurs through contact with or the experience of pure consciousness.[37] Another view suggests that transcendence can occur through an experience of the sacred as the socially influenced conception of the ultimate reality, truth or God[38], and its expression in one's cognitive, affective and behavioural functioning.

Similarly, A.B. Newberg and D. Monti note that spirituality involves cognitive, emotional, behavioural and experiential outcomes of the exploration for the sacred.[39] The view of the sacred as an individual's perception of something divine or the fundamental truth or phenomenon in Newberg's and Monti's work seems to refer to the transcendent aspects, or aspects going beyond the physical or lower self.[40] With such interpretation, these criteria associated with spirituality also reflect a view of spirituality as a connection with or experience of the transcendent in the form of the sacred. As the phenomena referred to by the term 'sacred' include God[41] and divine[42], spirituality can be viewed as also having a relationship with divinity and the almighty.

The above discussion suggests that spirituality or spiritual development involves going beyond self-interests and being harmoniously connected to others in terms of functioning in relation to the world, and it also involves having a connection with God or the divine. These two forms could be respectively referred to as the horizontal dimension and vertical dimension of spirituality.

∽

Thus, two views of spirituality seem to be reflected in scientific literature. One view suggests that spirituality is the transcendence of the material and physical self. Another view suggests that spirituality is the connection with the higher self, viewed as some conception of the sacred or pure consciousness. These two forms of spirituality seem to have the common outcome of peace and tranquillity. For example, spiritual goals or values have been found to be positively associated with well-being.[43] As the adoption of spiritual goals and values could reflect the transcendence of the material self, these findings suggest that spiritual experience and well-being are a consequence of transcending the material self. Spirituality is also conceived as a connection with or experience of pure consciousness that comes when the mind transcends its ordinary level.[44] Research findings indicate that the practice of transcendental meditation, which is a way of connecting with pure consciousness, is associated with the outcome of greater well-being.[45] Thus, both approaches to spirituality—transcendence of the material self, and connection with the higher self or pure consciousness—have the common outcome of enhanced well-being.

The above description suggests that a lack of transcendence beyond the material self results in lower well-being. This is consistent with the research findings noted by T. Kasser, which suggest that the pursuit of higher levels of materialistic goals or materialistic values is associated with higher levels of depression, anxiety, sadness, frustration and anger.[46] Further, the view reflected in the above description is that the experience of the transcendent requires going beyond or transcending the material self or material self-interests. This is consistent with the research findings noted by Kasser, suggesting that materialistic goals or values and spiritual goals or values are incompatible.[47] This suggests that to experience the transcendent, it is necessary to go beyond the material self or materialistic goals.

Further, there seems to be a relationship between these two terms of transcendence. For example, a connection with pure consciousness brings about positive functioning.[48] It is likely that the positive functioning may get expressed through behaviours such as generosity and prosocial behaviour, which reflect transcendence of the physical or material self. These inferences suggest that a connection with the higher self results in transcendence of the physical or material self, or self-interests. In other words, progress along the vertical dimension of transcendence results in progress in the horizontal dimension too.

It is also plausible that the transcendence of the material self facilitates a connection with the higher self or pure consciousness. For example, D.P. Heaton, J. Schmidt-Wilk and F. Travis suggest that the experience of pure consciousness is an experience of the absence of ordinary objects and the associated cognitive, perceptual or emotional elements.[49] As one's objects of perception, thoughts, etc., are likely to reflect material or self-centred concerns, and going beyond these is a prerequisite for connection with pure consciousness, it implies that going beyond material concerns can facilitate a connection with or experience of pure consciousness. Further, Fry suggests that one of the spirituality-based ways to experience God is through honouring one's duties.[50] Honouring one's duties reflects going beyond material self-interests. This suggests that advancement in the horizontal dimension of transcendence can facilitate progress in the vertical dimension of transcendence as well. Thus, the horizontal and vertical dimensions of transcendence can have a mutually reinforcing relationship—in that development along one facilitates development along the other.

C.H. Liu and P.J. Robertson view spirituality as a particular form of identity, suggesting that identities can be placed on a continuum from self-focused to transcendent-focused, and that the transcendent-focused identity reflects the highest level on the spirituality continuum.[51] This also implies that approaching a transcendent-focused identity requires moving away from the self-focused identity.

The vertical and horizontal dimensions of transcendence reflect, respectively, a connection with the higher self or entity such as the sacred or God, and with others in the world.

Both the connection with God and connectedness with living beings in the world, as components of spirituality, are reflected in the definition of spirituality by L. Bouckaert and L. Zsolnai as a variously manifesting exploration process for life's profound meaning by an individual that can link the individual to not only living beings but also God.[52] Consistent with this, Fry notes that spirituality involves an individual's relationship with a greater—and possibly divine—entity and the resulting influences on the individual's life functioning.[53]

One expression of horizontal transcendence is in the form of higher values in one's functioning. The literature suggests spirituality as a process and state of going beyond or transcending the physical or material self, and experiencing the transcendent self and the expression of such transcendent experience in one's functioning in various domains such as cognitions, emotions and behaviours.[54] One way of going beyond material self-interests while operating in the world is to adopt moral values or higher values in one's functioning. The centrality of values in spirituality is reflected in the view of R.W. Kolodinsky, R.A. Giacalone and C.L. Jurkiewicz who suggest that individual spirituality is characterized by the spectrum of spiritual values of an individual.[55] That spirituality involves higher values is also reflected by Fry, who suggests that a spiritually refined individual's expression of spirituality can consist of certain values that reflect a refined inner self, and that which can make oneself and others happy.[56] This also suggests that spirituality is reflected in bringing happiness to all, including oneself. Consistent with this, Fry suggests that selfless love—characterized by a commitment to others' welfare—is a feature common to spirituality and religion.[57]

A similar view is reflected in Bouckaert and Zsolnai who note that two of the common components of spirituality are: a quest for higher values that elevate an individual beyond self-serving functioning and an empathetic orientation toward living entities.[58] Further, Fry mentions the notion of a calling as another form of transcendence in one's functioning in the world, and that a person's pursuit of a calling does good to others and can facilitate the person's transcendence.[59] Thus, adoption of higher values in one's functioning and doing good to others or in the world through one's work is another manifestation of the horizontal dimension of spirituality.

The preceding description of the literature on spirituality suggests that spirituality involves both a vertical dimension and a horizontal dimension. Maintaining a connection with the divine, God, the higher self, or in general with the sacred is the vertical dimension of spirituality. Connectedness with others, devotion to the interests of others, making positive contributions to others, and the adoption of universal values, moral values or higher values are some of the manifestations of spirituality in one's functioning in the world, and constitute the horizontal dimension of spirituality.

The presence of these aspects of the vertical and horizontal dimensions of spirituality in Baai's life and functioning is outlined below.

The Vertical Dimension of Transcendence in Baai's life

Throughout her life, Baai was engaged in the pursuit of God. She would listen in rapture to scriptures being read in the village temple. These reading sessions would usually take place at night so that people could attend those after having completed their day's work. Baai would not have had time for dinner before the scripture-reading session because she would have had a lot on her plate between managing and cooking for a large family, and working as a field labourer. She would only have dinner after returning home late at night—such was her dedication to religious pursuits.

Whenever Baai narrated incidents of God's glories based on her listening of the scriptures, she would narrate them with great devotion, in a manner as though she had witnessed them. For example, one of the scriptures narrates the devotional triumphs and glories of God's devotees, and is also known as the triumphs of devotion (*bhakti vijaya*). Baai would narrate the ordeals and triumphs of the devotees from this scripture in detail and with a sense of absorption, as though she had witnessed what she was narrating. She would also feel deeply engrossed in listening to kirtans. In one such kirtan, she recounted that she was not only hearing the words but was also actually seeing God's glories unfolding before her eyes. Baai requested the religious person who had delivered that kirtan to be her *guru* (a spiritual mentor and guide), and he accepted the request by the simple act of giving her a rosary. Beyond this simple act, Baai's spiritual journey mostly remained independent of him, except for paying obeisance to him once a year when he occasionally visited her village.

Going on pilgrimages in her middle age also reflected her intense yearning to seek a connection with God. The pilgrimages meant many sacrifices and hardships, from loss of wages to the cost of travelling. Perhaps, Baai accepted all such hardships because she received the bliss of a connection with the divine.

During her old age, Baai took part in group spiritual

activities such as bhajans and paaraayan. She also devoted time to personal spiritual practices such as dev pooja, japa, prayers and aarati. It was only after the age of about 60, when she was freed from her daily strenuous routine, that she could devote time to sit down quietly to practise japa. By the time Baai reached old age, she had attained a close contact with God, and thus during her spiritual practises she seemed to go into a trance-like state.

Baai's connection with God was strengthened all through her life, so much so that by old age she could transcend the miseries of physical decay, pain, and any concerns about death. She had developed a near complete identification with the transcendent, and hence a sense of detachment from her physical self. Thus, she had reached the destination point along the vertical dimension of spirituality; in other words, she had attained the transcendent state that represents the stage of liberation. Her life shows that one can experience God while living an ordinary life and performing daily work activities.

The Horizontal Dimension of Transcendence in Baai's Life

Baai's sense of connection with others reflected her selfless love (which Fry suggests is the commitment to others' welfare[60]). Baai would say that there is an element of the divine in everyone, and hence one should not do anything that may cause harm to others. Rather, one should empathize with others and sense their sufferings and sorrows ('*itarancha jeev jaanava*').

One example of Baai's connectedness with others is when she worked in the hostel mess. Sensing the need of students who were away from their homes and parents, she tried to shower them with affection, food and nourishment with no thought for material reward. Throughout her life, groups of women were drawn to Baai's sense of connectedness, and her ability to sense their suffering and fulfil their needs—from the time she did brick-laying work as a child, to when she worked on fields as an agricultural labourer, to when she became old and lived in a society flat in Pune. This expression of the awareness that God dwells in all—which manifested in her behaviour toward others as the horizontal dimension of transcendence—possibly facilitated her vertical transcendence and connection with God.

Doing well to others through one's work is a form of transcendence and is reflected in the notion of 'calling'.[61] Baai made several contributions to others throughout her lifetime, especially to her children. And when she became too old to physically contribute and care for them, she expressed concern for them through prayers and her blessings.

Baai also rendered service to her husband. When he became ill and gradually lost his income-earning capability, Baai alone shouldered the responsibility for the livelihood of the entire family. During the old age and ill health of her father-in-law, Baai gave him affection, care and nursing. As mentioned earlier, the relief her father-in-law received through her care for him was such that he would lean his old and emaciated head on her shoulder, and weep while saying that to him Baai was almost like his mother.

Baai also rendered care and service to her mother-in-law in many ways. When her mother-in-law became old and could not take part in cooking, Baai would cook delicious food, which the children would hurriedly feast on. Baai would take out some quantity of these delicious items from the common food storage container and keep them in small containers, which she would hide from the children and save for her old mother-in-law. In the early years of her marriage, Baai made sure not to report any of her hardships at her in-laws' house, as she knew this would have given her mother immense grief at not being able to protect her. In this way, she rendered service to her mother.

Her life conveys that one does not necessarily need to do anything beyond one's daily chores and duties to render service to God. This is strikingly in contrast to some religious preachers who appeal to people to donate wealth as a way of service. Baai's humility and sense of obedience to God's order, in accepting one's circumstances and rendering service in the given circumstances as per the requirements of others, was her calling.

∽

Expression of higher values, spiritual values, universal values, or values that go beyond an ego-centric orientation is one dimension of spirituality, as per the literature described in the early part of this chapter. Such values include doing well to others and avoiding harm, and these reflect attainment of self-transcendence and a sense of connectedness with others. Baai's life was an embodiment of several higher values such as courage, hard work, diligence, persistence, endurance, honesty, truthfulness, contentment, humility, tolerance, non-violence, forgiveness, empathy, compassion and altruism.

Baai faced several adversities throughout most of her life with courage. She practised tremendous hard work in mobilizing several honest ways of earning a livelihood for her family, including back-breaking work such as breaking stones with a hammer at a quarry in torrid summer. Honesty is one of the higher values that Baai upheld in her life. For example, while breaking stones at a quarry, she abstained from practices such as over-reporting the volume of stone chips broken by her.

She also upheld the value of non-violence. In her adult years, Baai did not hurt anyone either through her words or through her actions. Any violent intent itself seemed to be absent in her. Rather, she exercised the values of endurance and tolerance to uphold her determination to not cause harm to anyone. For example, she not only showed forgiveness towards her father-in-law for the ill-treatment she had received from him when she was a child, but also nursed him with immense kindness and compassion during his ill health and old age.

GLEANINGS

- Spirituality, in scientific literature, is characterized by transcendence along a vertical dimension and a horizontal dimension.
- Vertical transcendence involves the process and attainment of a connection with the sacred element, labelled variously as pure consciousness, the divine, or God.
- Horizontal transcendence involves maintaining a connection with and contributing to others. It also involves practising spiritual or higher values, including personal spiritual values such as honesty, courage, determination, diligence and endurance, and interpersonal spiritual

values such as non-violence, tolerance, forgiveness and compassion. The horizontal and vertical aspects of transcendence strengthen each other, and hence, progress along one dimension facilitates progress along the other.

- Baai achieved vertical transcendence through a simple yet profound connection with God in her everyday life. Her various simple spiritual practices integrated in her everyday functioning expressed faith in, awareness of, and reliance on God's presence and strength.
- In her pursuit of horizontal transcendence, Baai prioritized connection with and contribution to others, embodying positive interpersonal values and fulfilment of life duties regardless of circumstances. She didn't wait for ideal conditions but engaged fully within her existing relationships.
- Her life illustrates that spiritual fulfilment doesn't demand discipleship or organized service. Instead, belief in God, understanding divine principles, and embodying them in everyday functioning suffice. Baai's innate faith and capacity for compassion enabled her to live by these principles effortlessly.
- Contrary to some religious organizations and social movements that prescribe specific paths to transcendence, Baai's life exemplifies a natural, ongoing process of transcendence or spiritual development. Living an ordinary life with a certain type of everyday functioning facilitated her connection with God and her contribution to others, enhancing her transcendence both vertically and horizontally, without deliberate spiritual exercises separated from everyday life or extraordinary efforts.

10
A View Based on the Scriptures

In Hindu religion, Shrimad Bhagavad Gita is the essence of the Vedic scriptures. Bhagavad Gita is also known as Gitopanisad. It is the essence of Vedic knowledge and one of the most important Upanishads in Vedic literature.[1] The significance of Shrimad Bhagavad Gita is reflected in the assessment of Thomas Merton, who notes, 'The Gita can be seen as the main literary support for the great religious civilization of India, the oldest surviving culture in the world.'[2] Similarly, Dr Geddes MacGregor notes, 'No work in all Indian literature is more quoted, because none is better loved in the West than Bhagavad Gita.'[3]

The verses from this significant Vedic scripture of Shrimad Bhagavad Gita are commented upon and elaborated in *Dnyaneshwari*, which was originally named 'Bhavartha Deepika', and which can be approximately interpreted as the light on to the essence of meaning. In the following part, *Dnyaneshwari* is mainly used as a basis for the scripture-based view of spirituality. To supplement this, insights from a few saints and references to Shrimad Bhagavad Gita are also occasionally used.

Among the various ways of attaining yoga, four main paths are mentioned in *Dnyaneshwari* and Shrimad Bhagavad Gita:

- *Saankhya yoga/dnyaan yoga* is about seeking union with God through knowledge about God's design for and operation in the world, and about one's real nature.
- Karma yoga is about seeking union with God by doing one's noble God-ordained duties without a sense of ego and expectation of sensual outcomes.
- *Dhyaan yoga* is about seeking union with God through the removal of the mind from the material world so that the mind is cleared of material concerns, the intellect is freed from planning material outcomes, and thus the intellect is purified enough to comprehend and experience God or the divine element within.
- Bhakti yoga is about seeking union with God by connecting the mind with God through various means, such as maintaining continual remembrance of God, obeying God's principles (such as mercy and truthfulness), refraining from unethical behaviour, being egoless, dedicating all deeds to God, and relinquishing the outcomes of one's deeds.

Two of these four paths were clearly visible in Baai's life: karma yoga and bhakti yoga.

Karma Yoga in Baai's Life

The essence of karma yoga includes aspects such as steadying one's intellect in God and stopping it from getting into the attachment–aversion duality, remaining equanimous in situations that could cause either happiness or sorrow, performing one's God-ordained duties, avoiding the egoistic position of being the doer of the work, and also offering one's work to God while relinquishing the outcomes of one's work. Baai acknowledged and fulfilled her duties to many people in her life. Some of these duties imposed considerable hardships and suffering on her. Yet, she performed all the duties without getting into the attachment–aversion duality; neither did she feel attached to those duties that were easy and pleasant, nor did she feel averse to those duties that were unpleasant and full of hardship.

In early childhood, the circumstances of Baai's maternal family imposed on her the duty of supplementing the family's earnings, which she diligently performed. Then, when she came to her in-laws in early childhood, Baai performed the duty of obeying her mother's advice of enduring and not retaliating to the ill-treatment meted out to her, and also the duty of complying with every demand of physical labour imposed on her by her in-laws. Thereafter, she performed the duty of supplementing the income and supporting the livelihood of her in-laws. Years later, she also accepted the duty of rearing her children and making education accessible to them. In her old age, she accepted a marginal and subservient role in the families of her sons, facilitated the strengthening of their families, and reared their children.

For fulfilling such duties toward her family members, she had to accept strenuous work such as working as a daily agriculture labourer in distant farms, working on rearing cattle, working as a cook in the kitchen of a hostel, and working in a quarry. Baai uncomplainingly, diligently and honestly performed all such duties. Even while doing challenging work, for example cooking in the students' hostel and being constantly exposed to the fumes and smoke from the chullah, she continuously remembered God and focused on serving.

Baai did not seek recognition, praise, comfort or reciprocation from others for her work. Nor did she neglect the work because it was strenuous or had no material gains for her. Rather, she diligently performed any work as her duty. While doing so, she chanted God's holy name. Such performance of daily tasks and constant remembrance of God is a path of spiritual development outlined by Sant Shri Eknath Ji Maharaj. Some of the abhangas of Sant Shri Eknath Ji Maharaj suggest that performing daily routine deeds (*nitya karma*) and event-based occasional (*naimittik*) work purifies the mind or consciousness (*chitta*), and that such devotion to God steadies/stabilizes the mind or consciousness.[4] Thus, neatly performing the daily and event-based occasional work—which Baai continued to do all her life—and continual remembrance of God throughout Baai's life formed a lifelong and natural means of spiritual development and God-realization for her.

Dnyaneshwari[5] suggests that one's God-ordained duties should not be relinquished, and one should quietly endure whatever accrues while appropriately carrying out these duties. Thus, Baai accepted all her work as God-ordained work and maintained equanimity even when she faced adverse consequences. *Dnyaneshwari* suggests that if one's intellect is illuminated in such a way that one performs work without expecting any outcome, then one's fear of the material world vanishes, implying that one is liberated from materialistic entanglements.[6] *Dnyaneshwari* suggests that performing all work that comes one's way as if it were a part of God's wish (*svakarma* or *vihit karma*) is good for one's liberation, and therefore should not be neglected or abandoned. Rather, one should perform God-ordained work without longing for the outcome; one should do good work (*satkriya*) without seeking any materialistic pleasure from it and should not do unethical work (*kukarma*).[7]

Baai always refrained from unethical work. She neither neglected God-ordained work nor sought any material pleasures. In this way, Baai's karma yoga continued throughout her life. *Dnyaneshwari*[8] suggests that by maintaining a connection with God, one should carefully do one's work without any expectation. One should not feel elated when the work fructifies or angry if it does not. When the work accomplished by the self is dedicated to God, it becomes complete. This way of remaining equanimous, while doing good or God-ordained work, is an excellent state of yoga.

Dnyaneshwari further suggests that the equanimity of mind and the alignment of mind and intellect itself are yoga.[9] Put simply, when the mind is liberated from desires, when actions aren't driven by cravings, when the intellect recognizes that actions are divinely ordained, and when the mind remains balanced regardless of outcomes, then engaging in work with such harmony between mind and intellect fosters the practice of yoga. *Dnyaneshwari* suggests that when the delusion of doing work for the fulfilment of desire disappears, and thereby when work is performed as obedience of God's wish, then detachment emerges, leading to self-realization (that the self itself is divine).[10]

Baai performed her work as God-ordained duty without seeking rewards and taking credit for completing the work. As a result, she had earned detachment, liberation from the material self, and self-knowledge through her work, which had transformed into karma yoga (union with God through work).

With one's intellect stabilized in God, one is freed of the oscillations of joy and sadness, desires, anger and fear. Further, *Dnyaneshwari* suggests that the person who wishes well for others regardless of whether they are evolved or fallen, who remains equanimous in the occurrence of both negative and positive outcomes, and who has self-knowledge, is the one whose intellect is connected with God.[11] Baai wished well for all regardless of their status and standing, and she even wished well for those who hurt her. Baai also preserved her courage and equanimity in the face of both positive and negative outcomes, and thus her intellect had a connection with God throughout her life.

Dnyaneshwari mentions ways of and obstacles in stabilizing one's intellect in God, and the process through which one reaches one's complete, content and peace-filled self.[12] For reaching the state in which one's intellect is stabilized in God (*sthit-pradnya*), one has to restrain one's senses from the objects of sensual pleasures. However, such restraint does not succeed if the desire for the taste of objects of sensual pleasures remains in one's mind. When this happens, the mind develops attachment to the objects of sensual pleasures, and experiences anger when the objects are not available. And because of anger one loses happiness and peace.

Thus, when senses are engaged in deriving sensual pleasures, the mind gets drawn to enjoying these, and one's intellect gets drawn into forming plans to obtain more sensual pleasures. In order to prevent the mind from getting carried away by senses, it is necessary to remove from the mind the desires for sensual pleasures, and this can happen when the mind experiences peace through its union with God/self because the God/self is complete, content and peace-filled. Therefore, not only do the senses need to be restrained from the objects of sensual pleasures, but also simultaneously the mind needs to be connected with God. Thus, with the mind being freed from the craving for sensual pleasures, one's intellect gets stabilized in God. Once the mind experiences peace because of its union with God/self, then, even while being surrounded by sense objects, the mind does not get carried away towards the pleasures of these objects. Thus, the peace coming from the union with peace-filled self/God eliminates the desire for and downfall in the sensual pleasures, even when one is in contact with such objects.

This process involving sense objects, senses, mind, intellect, sensual pleasures and peace explains why spiritual aspirants practise a regimen in which they abstain from consuming supposedly desire-enhancing food items such as garlic, onion, certain spices, tea and coffee, and from lively social engagements. Baai lived an ordinary and simple life full of many social duties, social engagements, and other activities regarded by her as obedience to the design or order of God, and hence everything was done as an acceptance of God's wish and not for the pursuit of desire.

Thus, her life was one of karma yoga, or union with God through every act. Baai's remembrance and contemplation of God, her quiet repetition and uttering of God's divine name, her engagement in other activities such as listening to scriptures, and her performance of life's duties as the fulfilment of God's duties continued even without having to maintain the restrained type of living that spiritual aspirants tend to adopt. This is consistent with abhanga number 870 of Sant Shri Tukaram Ji Maharaj: one should neither give up food nor go and dwell in isolation in forests, one should neither renounce nor get locked in indulgence; rather, one should maintain a remembrance of God while going through the motions of life.[13] In other words, one can engage in indulgence in life's pleasures as long as the remembrance of God does not cease. Similarly, Sant Shri Tukaram Ji Maharaj says (abhanga number 3,003)[14] that he neither did japa, nor performed *tapa* (self-purifying living or conduct or prolonged regimented practice, spiritual austerities or penances), nor offered water in worship to God; rather, he pleaded with God and maintained constant remembrance of God.

Furthermore, Sant Shri Tukaram Ji Maharaj says (in abhanga number 3,641) that one who chants God's holy name while walking, eating, doing one's work, and doing every form of abstinence or indulgence—in effect, one who has performed all holy offerings to God (*yagna*) and observed fasts—is purified, is freed of the bondages of his deeds, has attained peace and happiness, and is liberated.[15] The essence of these abhangas is that a constant connection with God, and doing every deed in God's name, leads to union with God. This essence characterized Baai's life and thus she did not require extensive and regimented spiritual practices that put restrictions on food intake or social interactions.

Verse 70 from Chapter 2 of Bhagavad Gita suggests that like an ocean that is not disturbed because of various rivers entering into it, a person whose mind does not get contaminated by sensual pleasures attains peace.[16] *Dnyaneshwari* suggests that one who experiences the peace of God/self has his mind fixed in God, and he then gets rid of his ego, leaves all desires, and remains in the world as if he is a part of the world.[17] Verse 71 from Chapter 2 of Bhagavad Gita suggests that the one who has control over desires, attachment and ego attains peace.[18] Thus, the mind-contaminating or mind-disturbing effects—which things such as delicious or spicy food, and social engagements could probably have—did not affect Baai because her mind was absorbed in God. Baai did so much work with a feeling that it was for the fulfilment of God-ordained duties that her mind did not have any capacity left for seeking the fulfilment of desire. Thus, Baai, freed from desires and ego, remained in union with God and at peace.

Dnyaneshwari suggests that performing good deeds or God-ordained work is necessary for attaining the state in which all work ceases.[19] This suggests that by doing God-ordained work, one reaches the state of self-realization and hence the need for doing any deed for attaining material pleasure does not remain. *Dnyaneshwari* further suggests that one who remains in union with God, and does God-ordained work without desires or attachments, is liberated and is a *yogi* (one who is in union with God).[20] Therefore, one should discipline the mind, be pure within, and then let the organs of action perform worldly duties.

The meaning of Verse 7 from Chapter 3 of Bhagavad Gita suggests that one who controls his senses by the mind, does not get attached to sensual pleasures, and applies all the senses in the enactment of karma yoga is a great person.[21] *Dnyaneshwari* suggests that God-ordained work, when done without the objective of fulfilling material desires, is a source of liberation and is a continual offering to God.[22] Hence, there is no bondage or sin associated with it. Baai diligently fulfilled her God-ordained duties and outwardly lived a life similar to others. Yet, the distinction lay in her perception of these tasks as divine obligations. Consequently, she did not perceive herself as the sole actor in her endeavours, refrained from pursuing sensual gratification as a result of her work, and maintained a constant focus on God within her thoughts.

Dnyaneshwari suggests that when one's mind is free of desires, then one becomes free of any attachments to the objects of sensual pleasure, without even having to distance oneself from the objects or without restraining the senses.[23] Similarly, the text also suggests that one should not restrain the senses or sever engagements that lead to worldly joys but should follow the duties coming from one's ancestry (or tradition), refrain from unethical deeds, and have happiness in life. One should relinquish the sense of being the doer of all deeds and should offer all deeds to God.[24] These verses also suggest that such devout orientation leads one to unite with God.

These verses also suggest that one should purify and regulate the mind, perform God-ordained duties, refrain from viewing oneself as the doer of one's work, and offer one's deeds to God. Thus, Baai did not have to eliminate items such as spices, onion, garlic and tea (which strengthen the senses) nor reduce delicious food from her diet because her mind was clean and connected to God, and thus her senses could not pull her mind into the objects of sensual pleasure. This way, Baai's mind was engaged in God, cleansed and pure, and it did not get attached to objects of sensual pleasure despite their presence in her life. Thus, while living an ordinary life, Baai was liberated and had progressed toward attaining union with God.

Other verses from *Dnyaneshwari* also suggest a similar view, that with a purified mind the restraining of senses becomes unnecessary. For example, *Dnyaneshwari* suggests that living an ordinary life but eliminating a sense of attachment to the outcomes of one's deeds and removing from the mind the plans for seeking sensual pleasures (*sankalpa*) itself is the state of renunciation of the material world (*sanyaas*) and union with God (yoga).[25] Similarly, it further suggests that doing one's God-ordained duty is a way of attaining fulfilment and hence no other abstinence or pilgrimage is required.[26]

Dnyaneshwari suggests that being desireless and performing God-ordained duties takes one to self-realization or liberation.[27] It also suggests that just as a desire-seeking person works vigorously for desire fulfilment, so too the self-realized person should work vigorously for doing work for the benefit of the world.[28] This suggests that no duty or work remains obligatory for the self-realized person, but rather the person should continue to vigorously do the work for the benefit of the world. It was while vigorously and wholeheartedly doing the God-ordained duties in a desireless manner and while doing good to others that Baai's union with God developed.

The following process emerges from Chapters 2 and 3 of *Dnyaneshwari*, which elaborate on different forms of karma yoga. The desire (*kaam*) occupies the senses, mind and intellect. Even when the senses are kept away from the objects of sensual pleasure, the taste for sensual pleasures remains in the mind. Even a fleeting encounter of the senses with objects of sensual pleasure can lure the mind into a spiral of attachment to such objects, triggering anger, attachment–aversion (*raag–dvesh*) dualities, memory lapses, agitation, loss of peace, and ultimately destruction. Controlling the senses alone isn't sufficient. However, when one experiences peace from the self or God through divine union, the mind loses interest in sensual pleasures and becomes desireless. At that point, the senses can't lure the desireless mind into indulgence. Thus, the recommended approach is to divert the senses from sensual objects while engaging the mind in contemplation of the self or God simultaneously.

When the peace of the self or God is experienced by contact and experience of the self or God, then one can remain unaffected even when surrounded by objects of sensual pleasure—just as an ocean is unaffected by the entrance of several rivers into it. Karma yoga facilitates this because as the senses are engaged in the God-ordained work, they do not have an opportunity to seek sensual pleasures; and as the fruits of and credit for the outcome of work is offered to God, and an awareness is maintained that God has got the work done, the mind is simultaneously engaged in God/self.

Thus, keeping senses away from the objects of sensual pleasures and engaging the mind in God/self occur simultaneously in karma yoga. Karma yoga frees the mind from attachment to or desire of sensual pleasures, and makes the mind desireless (*vairagya*, which is dispassion or detachment from the objects of sensual or material pleasure). This is the main step in attaining liberation, peace and union with God. *Dnyaneshwari*'s verses from Chapters 2, 3, 12 and 18 also suggest this role of vairagya. Other forms of spiritual practices also result in vairagya. For example, *Dnyaneshwari* suggests that engaging the mind in God for some moments during the day removes the mind from the objects of sensual pleasures, and allows it to dwell in the divine self/God and provides it divine happiness; and thus the mind slowly disengages from sensual pleasures and attains union with God.[29]

Baai continually remembered God and thus it is likely that Baai's mind received the divine happiness, which helped her survive through life's adversities and lowered her desires for sensual pleasures. Thus, she was not carried away by the desires of the mind, remained focused on doing God-ordained duties without having a sense of being the doer, offered her works to God, constantly remembered God in her mind, and refrained from unethical deeds and pursuit of sensual pleasures that would distract her from doing God-ordained duties. Hence, Baai's karma yoga occurred through her work in the service of those around her and through her fulfilment of many duties to others in her family and community.

Overall, Baai worked hard and unceasingly all through her life on fulfilling her worldly responsibilities, and viewed them as God-ordained duties for which various terms such as vihit, satkriya, *satkarma*, svakarma and *swadharma* are used in *Dnyaneshwari*. She upheld her ethicality in doing her duties and thus refrained from inappropriate deeds (kukarma). She maintained her faith that her work got done by God, and she dedicated her work and their outcomes to God.[30] With Baai's hectic engagement in God-ordained duties, at least till the late middle phase of her life, she did not have time or energy left to seek desire satiation, as she was immersed in fulfilling her duties, and thus duty-fulfilment rather than sense-indulgence was the way of her life. Both karma yoga and bhakti yoga were apparent in Baai's life and functioning. With such a purified mind, she continued to discover and fulfil many forms of duties throughout her life. For example, she mobilized immense energy to fulfil several duties through a hectic routine containing several strenuous activities with less sleep and low-quality nutrition through the early and middle phases of her life.

Even in her old age, when she could not contribute to others through her physical efforts, she discovered and fulfilled duties such as helping others with her wisdom and advice. Such greater pursuit of altruistic work and greater availability of energy because of a purified mind is noted in *Dnyaneshwari*. The text suggests that when a person performs God-ordained duties for divine bliss without bothering about bodily pleasures, then laziness and sleep disappear, hunger is not sensed, energy or enthusiasm increases, desire for sensual pleasures disappears, body-centred thinking (*deha buddhi*) weakens, and the happiness from performing God-ordained duties increases.[31] This seems to explain how Baai could, in the early and middle phases of her life, perform strenuous work as God-ordained duties, and remain energetic despite a hectic and strenuous routine, little rest, and inadequate nutrition. Possibly, the experience of divine bliss helped Baai to endure material hardships, and physical pain associated with the hardships and severe adversities. The capacity to endure physical pain, deprivations and adversities remained with Baai all through her life. This capacity was with her even in her disease-ridden physical condition during the last few days of her stay on this planet.

Thus, she continued to discover and fulfil God-ordained duties, endured physical pain and deprivations, remained equanimous in adverse circumstances, endured sufferings due to changes in life stages, and coped with the pains of the body's natural decline and ageing. Throughout, Baai maintained a constant connection with God through remembrance and japa of God's name, listening to and reflecting on scriptures, and seeing God in others. Thus, many forms of prolonged and regimented spiritual practices (sadhana) naturally became integral to Baai's life, contributing to her experience of God dwelling within her, as God does in every creature. These practices led her to a sense of liberation from her body and its sufferings, to an experience of continual peace, and to a serene acceptance of her departure from this world. The conventional spiritual practices—such as meditation, observance of a specific regimen of food, regular pilgrimage, regular visits to temples, prolonged or recurring observance of fasts—were not the main components of Baai's spiritual journey. Rather, she attained union with God by ethically doing good work as service to God, offering the outcomes of the work to God, and by continually connecting with God.

God-ordained duties done in a diligent and ethical manner constitute service to God. *Dnyaneshwari* suggests that those who wish to attain liberation need to perform God-ordained work or good deeds.[32] It also suggests that for the purification of the mind, which possibly implies removal of desires, good deeds are like a pilgrimage. It further suggests that pilgrimages cleanse the external body while good deeds purify one's mind, and also states that while good deeds cleanse the mind, knowledge illuminates it.

Chapter 18 of *Dnyaneshwari* also outlines the mechanisms through which good deeds purify the mind and lead to self-realization (experience of the spiritual self within) and liberation (detachment from the physical self and its sufferings). It indicates that good deeds reduce the desire for sensual pleasures and enhance liking for good deeds. Thus, good deeds weaken desire for sensual pleasures, lower the attraction toward objects of sensual pleasure, weaken the view of oneself as the physical body, and provide joy. Additionally, with weakened attraction toward objects of sensual pleasure, attraction or devotion to God intensifies and spiritual joy emerges. Detachment from the objects of sensual pleasures and detachment from the physical self (mukti or moksha), which is liberation, seem to occur in succession.

Bhakti Yoga in Baai's Life

Broadly, bhakti yoga involves keeping the mind (chitta) engaged in God. *Dnyaneshwari* suggests that a devotee (*bhakt*) is one who keeps all his senses engaged in God, and such a devotee is the supreme yogi (the one who has attained union with God).[33] Keeping all organs engaged in God implies using the organs to do God-ordained work, offering work to God, and believing that God got the work completed. Keeping the mind engaged in God implies not seeking the outcome of one's work, not harbouring desires for sensual pleasure in the mind, and continually remembering God. *Dnyaneshwari* also suggests the process of withdrawing the senses and mind from objects of sensual pleasures, and simultaneously engaging the mind in God as a way of attaining union with God.[34]

The text further suggests that doing God-ordained work, refraining from misdeeds or unethical deeds, offering such work to God, and using all organs/senses in God's service is a way of attaining unwavering union with God (*ananya yoga*).[35] This is quite similar to karma yoga, as elaborated in Chapters 2 and 3 of Bhagavad Gita, where it is suggested that one should not do unethical deeds but should do good deeds without expecting desire-fulfilment or any outcome from them, and whatever outcomes take place should be offered to God.

It may be noted that freeing the mind from the plans or resolutions for desire-fulfilment possibly implies decontamination or purification of mind. The Gita Press's Bhagavad Gita interprets Verses 6 and 7 from Chapter 12 as, 'Those God-engrossed (*matparayan*) devotees who offer all their deeds to Me, focus on My tangible form (*sagun*), maintain My remembrance and contemplate on Me, with an unwavering connection with Me, such God-engrossed devotees are liberated by Me from the world where physical bodies face death (they are helped to transcend the material perishable world).'[36]

Baai did all her work with a view to fulfil God-ordained duties, fulfilled most of them, did not engage in unethical work, offered the deeds to God, did not develop a sense of being the doer of the work she accomplished, did not allow her mind to waver on account of sensual desires, and maintained continual remembrance of God. Thus, bhakti yoga was evident in her life. *Dnyaneshwari* suggests that those who continually and undistractedly engage their mind in God become one with God and engage in devotion to God.[37] These various expressions suggest that continual engagement, with devotion of the mind in God, is a way of developing union with God.

Dnyaneshwari suggests that by engaging chitta (including mind and intellect) in God for some moments during the day, the chitta will taste the divine happiness or peace during those moments and will get detached from the objects of sensual pleasures, and gradually develop a union with God.[38]

Baai would maintain continual remembrance of God. For example, as mentioned previously, Baai would utter or silently repeat God's divine name when she used to lift and pound pestle in the mortar while powdering the ingredients to make spices for making curries in her job as a cook in the hostel kitchen. Baai would also intently listen to scriptures being read in the temple during night, and would reflect on their preachings.

Dnyaneshwari suggests that even if one cannot perform the practice of engaging chitta in God, then, without distancing from the worldly pleasures or restraining senses, all the actions happening from the self should be regarded as not caused by the self but should be viewed as being caused by God, and should be offered to God; one should place one's life in the service of God, and the *chitta vrutti* (the tendencies of mind) should be continually engaged in God.[39] With such an orientation attained by the end of one's life, one reaches God. It may be noted here that not distancing from the worldly pleasures or not restraining senses, as mentioned here, does not imply that it is advisable to have desires or fulfil sensual pleasures. These verses suggest that allowing senses to function and having pleasures is permissible only to the extent that they do not impair the continual engagement of chitta vrutti in God.

Thus, there is a clear limit on the functioning of senses and on allowing worldly pleasures, and even such limited pleasure-seeking actions are to be offered to God. This is similar to Sant Shri Tukaram Ji Maharaj's abhanga number 870[40], which suggests that one should neither abandon food intake nor dwell in isolation in a forest, and one should neither relinquish nor get entangled in sensual pleasures. Rather, one should maintain a continual remembrance of God and offer all to God. If engagement in sensual pleasures or worldly matters exceeds certain levels or forms, then the continual remembrance of God, and being able to offer all to God, is unlikely to occur because the mind will be engaged in a continual remembrance of the objects of sensual pleasure, and would develop a sense of being the doer of one's deeds.

Baai used to take meals to nourish her body so that it could be used to perform God-ordained duties. She used to take meals and some delicious food in order to satiate the God that dwells within (jeeva). Baai used to prepare delicious food so that the God in others was satiated, and others were nourished. She used to eat meals while viewing them as offerings (yagna) to God and even would say *Narayana-yeti-samarpayami* ('the food is offered to Lord Narayana'). In her old age, she would pay obeisance to the food plate before consuming the first morsel, and also after taking the last morsel of a meal. Baai would also say that taking food is like offering the fuel (*aahuti*) to the sacred fire within.

As reflected in *Dnyaneshwari*[41], Baai accepted all circumstances, roles, life patterns and duties that emerged at different stages of her life, and in each state remained content, fulfilled the God-ordained duties of that stage, did not develop the sense of being the doer of the work, offered her deeds to God, and maintained her mind's continual engagement with God as she tread the path of bhakti yoga.

Dnyaneshwari[42] suggests that even if one cannot regard every work as happening at the order or wish of God, and one cannot offer every work to God, one should relinquish the outcomes of work. It further suggests that the body, through its engagement in outcome-relinquished work, gets used for its own liberation. When the fruits of one's deeds are relinquished, a tendency for new deeds does not emerge. *Dnyaneshwari* suggests that enhancement in receiving sensual pleasures from the outcome of the deeds and development of a sense of being the doer are the bondage of the deeds.[43] These are a bondage because they create an urge to perform further deeds for fulfilling desires and for satisfying the ego.

Thus, deeds already performed give rise to new desire-driven and ego-driven needs. However, when outcomes of deeds are relinquished, this cycle of deeds giving rise to further desire-driven and ego-driven deeds stops. With such practice, self-knowledge emerges and the mind remains in the contemplation of God/self, the urge for doing work (for sensual pleasures or desire-fulfilment) disappears, and hence the outcomes of work can be easily relinquished and peace emerges. *Dnyaneshwari*, in Verse 136, suggests that a person's use of the body in doing work while relinquishing the outcomes of work liberates the person from a sense of being a physical body.[44]

Baai never expected or demanded outcomes of her work. For example, she served and nursed her father-in-law even when he was old, ailing and frail. In that state, Baai's father-in-law could not have provided any material benefits to Baai for her serving him, and there were no penalties for not serving him. Thus, her service to him was an act of performing a God-ordained duty towards a family member in need and also a God-ordained duty for relieving the pain of a creature who is an embodiment of God (jeeva). As another example, she reared and brought up her grandchildren but did not expect recognition for it, and did not demand that her grandchildren should serve her in her old age. Thus, this path of seeking union with God, which may be termed as *phala tyaagu yoga*[45] (union with God by relinquishing outcomes of work), a distinct form of bhakti yoga, was apparent in her life.

The description from Chapter 12 of *Dnyaneshwari*, which elaborates on verses in Chapter 12 of Shrimad Bhagavad Gita, suggests that bhakti yoga takes several forms. The first form involves continually engaging one's mind and intellect in God. The second form involves periodically engaging one's mind and intellect in God. The third form involves performing work for God, which possibly means doing God-ordained duties and serving the God dwelling in all, refraining from developing a sense of being the doer of one's work, and offering one's work to God. The fourth form involves relinquishing the outcomes of one's work.

Performing God-ordained duties and performing work for serving the God dwelling in all while keeping one's mind and intellect engaged in God is one part of bhakti yoga, which happened throughout Baai's life. The nature of God-ordained duties changed in different circumstances and phases of Baai's life. However, she understood the nature of God-ordained duties in each of her life circumstances and life phases, and sought to fulfil those duties. For example, in Baai's old age when her capacity for physical work had been lost, her family members were away from her, she was living alone, and had abundant time with help—which in the considerable preceding part of her life was taken away by the strenuous work—Baai accepted the God-ordained duty of providing her wisdom, advice and guidance to the neighbourhood community members, and helped them to solve their personal, familial and social problems, provided solace and joy to them, and created religious platforms and activities for them to experience a sense of connection with God, and thus to attain spiritual development.

Another way of practising bhakti yoga is to view God in all. *Dnyaneshwari* suggests that one form of having a union with God through devotion is to view God in every creature.[46] As bhakti yoga involves nurturing devotion to God, viewing God in all possibly implies having devotion to the well-being of all, or serving all with the view to express devotion to the God dwelling in all. Baai regarded God to be dwelling in every creature. Thus, at the end of a long summer when there was a drizzle, she would murmur and pray for the rain to be adequate so that grass would sprout, trees would become green, birds and animals would get some food to eat, and farmers could sow the fields and thus earn their livelihoods. When it rained in an untimely manner, Baai would feel sad and express her concern for farmers, saying that such untimely rain may damage crops and hence harm the farmers.

Maintaining a deliberate continuous connection of mind with God and avoiding the loss of this connection through certain attitudes characterizes bhakti yoga. This suggests that the essence of bhakti yoga involves connecting one's mind and intellect with God, and preventing the loss of this connection. This also requires certain divine virtues (*satguna*s) in one's functioning in all domains of life, including interpersonal conduct, because certain forms of functioning are consistent while certain other forms are inconsistent with the reality that God dwells in all creatures and pervades all existence. The satgunas reflect those forms of functioning that are consistent with the reality that God dwells in all creatures and pervades all of existence. Thus, practising satgunas constitutes devotion to God and facilitates bhakti yoga. Such divine virtues are described in Verses 13 to 19 of Chapter 12 of Bhagavad Gita.

These include a lack of envy, presence of friendliness and compassion, lack of attachment, lack of a sense of ego, presence of equanimity in instances of sorrow and happiness, forgiveness, contentment, firmness in the belief that one is a part of the divine, retention of mind and intellect in God, a lack of repulsion (*udvaig*), presence of harmlessness, freedom from the dualities of joy and sadness, fearlessness, freedom from agitation (tranquillity), absence of any expectations, keenness on maintaining purity of oneself, dispassion, freedom from misery, a lack of ego-based initiation of deeds, absence of joy from objects of sensual pleasure, absence of grief, absence of craving or material desire, a sense of relinquishing of both good (*shoobh*) and bad (*ashoobh*) deeds, treating friends and foes equally, maintaining equanimity in receiving respect and insult and in favourable and unfavourable circumstances, freedom from attachment, equanimity in criticism and praise, contemplation of God, and detachment from one's residence and steady intellect.[47]

Of these divine virtues, lack of attachment and sense of ego, presence of equanimity, contentment, belief in one's divine nature, a lack of repulsion, presence of fearlessness, tranquillity, purity, dispassion, freedom from misery, freedom from grief, a lack of material desires, contemplation of God, and steady intellect seem to have a personal focus, and can be referred to as personal divine virtues. Divine virtues such as lack of envy, presence of friendliness, compassion, forgiveness and harmlessness seem to have an interpersonal focus and can be referred to as interpersonal divine virtues. Additional divine virtues are listed in other chapters of Bhagavad Gita.

Quite a few of these satgunas (divine virtues) were present in Baai.[48] She did not envy anyone, demonstrated friendliness with and compassion for all creatures, including her cattle. Baai forgave even those who had hurt and harmed her, and her forgiveness for them was so genuine that she served, nursed and blessed even those who had caused grave harm to her. Baai had immense purity in thoughts, feelings, actions, her physical body and surroundings; thus, inner and outer purity and cleanliness was present in Baai. She did not take credit for the work that got done from her end, and for her coping with calamities; rather, she believed that God had got work done from her.

A lack of sense of ego for the work done by her was so clearly present in Baai that even during periods of serious calamities, she would thank God for having seen her through the day and would reaffirm to herself her faith that it was God who would also see her through the following day. Baai did not have cravings, remained free from misery and grief, and was equanimous, and thus had contentment despite various adverse circumstances such as extreme poverty, loss of several avenues to earn livelihood through labour during the famine period, lack of supportive or resourceful relatives, and simultaneously being confronted with multiple evolving responsibilities in her life. Thus, the very living of life became a means for Baai to attain union with God through devotion and through deeds.

Dnyaneshwari suggests that when one attains the knowledge of God, several qualities emerge in one's functioning, such as humility, lack of pride, and non-violence. One's speech gets filled with affection and kindness for others, and becomes truthful, soft, concise and sweet like ambrosia. One develops a sense of forgiveness, and one endures adversities without feeling that one is a sufferer. Griefless forgiveness suggests that one forgives others, and does not grieve the harm caused to oneself by others. One becomes free of doubt and greed, and becomes straightforward and transparent. One becomes pure in body and mind, possibly implying that one's thoughts, feelings and outward behaviour become pure, and hence one is not distracted by or does not crave for what is seen, heard or encountered, and does not develop a desire for sense-pleasure objects even while being in the midst of them. One does not get unsettled or lose courage or composure in the face of changing circumstances. One carefully protects one's mind from getting driven by the senses. One performs all God-ordained duties without developing a sense of being the doer. One remains equanimous in both favourable and unfavourable situations. And one develops unwavering devotion to God. Thus, one attains an experience of God and maintains an absorption in the spiritual knowledge.[49]

Baai exhibited several of these satgunas. For example, she did not have a false sense of pride or an inflated ego. Baai had practised complete forgiveness towards her in-laws, her children, and others in society because of whom she had suffered. She was straightforward and transparent, had composure, courage and equanimity, and also had immense control over her mind.

Dnyaneshwari suggests various divine qualities of one's mind and divine virtues[50], and Bhagavad Gita suggests that these divine qualities lead to liberation while the qualities of opposite nature lead to bondage or downfall.[51] The divine qualities mentioned in these verses include steadiness of one's intellect, charity, performing God-ordained duties without developing a sense of being the doer and without getting attached to the fruits from performing such duties, being selfless and self-sacrificing while doing charitable deeds, courtesy, straightforwardness, non-violence, truthfulness, mercy or compassion, a lack of attachment to sense objects even when surrounded by or in contact with such objects, a lack of enmity towards others, and selfless and self-sacrificing engagement in others' work.

Several of these satgunas were present in Baai as demonstrated in various episodes of her life. Her responses to the demands of various phases of her life reflect Baai having qualities such as a pure mind, charity, performance of God-ordained duties, courtesy, non-violence and other-benefitting deeds, truthfulness, compassion, mercy, non-attachment to the objects of sense pleasure, and selflessness and self-sacrifice while benefitting others. Thus, the qualities of mind and conduct that lead to liberation had developed in Baai and she was on the path to liberation because of her mode of functioning. Verses 14 to 16 in Chapter 17 of Bhagavad Gita describe tapa performed through body, speech and mind. Throughout her life, Baai manifested several of these divine virtues, including tapa.

Through the presence of several satgunas in her life and functioning, Baai's bhakti yoga is likely to have been facilitated. Bhakti (devotion to God) has a significant role in facilitating one's union with God.[52] Baai had faith in the existence of God. Once, she actually felt that she was seeing Lord Krishna and his divine play in Gokula (Lord Krishna's place of stay) while she was listening to a kirtan about Lord Krishna. *Dnyaneshwari* suggests that those who have devotion to God become free from enmity towards all and attain union with God.[53] Baai's devotion to God was intense and one could feel it when she used to describe God's divine plays and miracles; she was free from enmity and in fact had attained compassion for all creatures.

∽

The natural and continual occurrence of both karma yoga and bhakti yoga in Baai's life suggests that living life according to God's design and rules for life itself is a way of connecting with God, and attaining union with God. As Baai had been blessed with both these capacities, she did not need to follow several forms of prolonged and regimented spiritual practices, such as observing prolonged periods of fasting. Thus, her functioning through various stages of her life itself became a continual and prolonged sadhana, and through it, both karma yoga and bhakti yoga came naturally to her. Through such a way of living, Baai's mind attained union with God.

As her mind was already in union with God, she could immerse herself in continually chanting God's holy name, even at the stage of her leaving the physical body. Her death marked the moment of completion of her mind's already attained union with the divine consciousness. Such peaceful and serene passage from the physical body is reflected in *Dnyaneshwari*, which suggests that the one who knows and with a steady mind remembers the Brahman at the time of leaving the physical body, reaches the supreme self, and leaves the physical body as easily as the sound of a bell gradually diminishing, or the flame of a lamp gradually dimming and disappearing.[54]

Thus, Baai was chanting God's holy name, and her mind was in peace and serenity at the moment when her physical body stopped functioning. The finite living element of God or the divine in Baai's body, which has limited life and a bounded existence, had already got united and merged in the limitless and unbounded vast divinity. The liberation Baai had attained from her physical self reached its culmination when she attained perfection of her being in union with God or the divine consciousness.

GLEANINGS

- Karma yoga involves doing good deeds and God-ordained duties without developing a sense of being the doer, and without an attachment to the outcomes

of one's work. This also involves not doing unethical deeds or misdeeds.
- The practice of karma yoga results in vairagya. This weakened desire is a pathway to lower one's attachment to one's physical self, while heightening the urge for union with the divine, leading to self-realization, liberation and union with God.
- Bhakti yoga involves keeping one's organs, mind and intellect connected to God. This involves using one's organs to perform God-ordained duties, while not developing a sense of being the doer, renouncing the outcomes of one's work, offering one's work to God, and keeping one's mind in the remembrance of God.
- The practice of bhakti yoga also involves acknowledging the presence of God in all creatures and in the entire existence. This acknowledgement is reflected in the adoption of satgunas, which, in general, are: do good and avoid harm to others, reflect diminished ego, avoid entanglement in sense pleasures, uphold one's purity, and maintain a connection with God.
- The practice of bhakti yoga results in the mind sensing peace coming from its contact with the divine, and hence the mind's developing weakened desire for the objects of sensual pleasures (vairagya), which is a pathway for further progress towards union with God.
- Baai's engagement in worldly activities consisted of both karma yoga and bhakti yoga, which facilitated her spiritual journey and liberation from the physical body, and her eventual peaceful and serene leaving of the physical body.

11

Reflections on Practical Spirituality

The preceding parts of the book have acquainted us with Baai's story, and described various aspects of spirituality in Baai's life and functioning. The first of the two preceding chapters in this part has focused on how, from the viewpoints of scientific literature on spirituality, the features of Baai's life and functioning facilitated her spiritual development. The other chapter described how, from the viewpoints of scriptures, Baai's life and functioning facilitated her spiritual development. Now, this chapter outlines the features that any person can adopt in everyday functioning in order to facilitate one's spiritual development while living an ordinary life. These features, briefly described in this chapter, may be referred to as 'practical spirituality' or 'everyday spirituality'.

The view of spirituality emerging from the scientific literature as outlined in Chapter 9 implies that Baai embodied universal or noble values, reflecting her profound connection to all of existence. She found fulfilment in a positive life purpose, deriving meaning from fulfilling her various life duties. Baai sanctified every aspect of her existence and fully realized the innate human capacity for transcending the self. Ultimately, she achieved self-transcendence through her seemingly ordinary way of life.

The view of spirituality reflected in the scriptures, as outlined in Chapter 10, suggests that Baai's functioning in an ordinary life had facilitated her journey on the path of union with God through work (karma yoga) and through devotion to God (bhakti yoga). Her journey on this path had occurred while living an ordinary life that, till its middle phase, included unfavourable circumstances such as poverty, strenuous work, difficult responsibilities and adversities.

This brief sketch of Baai's life and the illustration of the spiritual elements in it, based on the scientific view of spirituality and the scripture-based view of spirituality, can serve as an aspirational guide to those who seek answers to questions about what practical spirituality is, how one can attain spiritual development while living an ordinary life, and what is the experience of peace and serenity that comes as an outcome of spiritual development.

This account of her life points out that the spiritual development process is routine, practical and feasible for everyone. Her life demonstrates that one can attain spiritual development while living an ordinary life full of multiple strenuous duties, a series of adversities, grief-inducing episodes, and changes in life circumstances. She is also an exemplar for how spiritual development occurs while living an ordinary life, which can help one serenely face, accept and deal with the natural ending stage of human life involving a decline in one's physical capabilities, emergence of various forms of ill health, and eventually death. Such service from this sketch of Baai's life would be an extension of several services Baai rendered while living her life. Here are some inferences and thoughts on how

Baai's practical spirituality can serve as a guidance for all.

∽

For an ordinary person, strengthening one's physical health involves being adequately healthy to fulfil one's life's duties and having resilience to deal with aspects such as weather changes, minor infections and occasional illnesses, rather than having to build up muscles like a keep-fit contestant. One may require occasional visits to a doctor when there are physical illnesses, and one may need to adjust the patterns of work, food intake and rest in response to changes in the weather and one's age. As an outcome of how well one looks after one's health in routine life, one's physical health gets strengthened or weakened over a period of time. For this, one does not need to disengage from routine life or become a recluse.

Just as attaining physical health does not necessarily mean attaining extraordinary physical strength, attaining spiritual development does not necessarily mean attaining any extraordinary spiritual powers. Rather, one can attain spiritual development by being able to remain contented, serene and peaceful in the face of life's inherent elements of unpredictability, challenges, life-stage-related changes, nature-ordained gradual weakening of one's physical strength and capabilities after a certain age, and certain occurrence of death. In other words, one does not need to disengage from routine life or become a recluse or an ascetic for facilitating one's spiritual development. Rather, one needs to simply function in certain ways, as reflected in various aspects of Baai's life and functioning, and their interpretations in light of scientific and scriptural literature explained in the preceding chapters of this book and summarized below. The features of such functioning in an ordinary life are briefly described below under two categories of horizontal and vertical dimensions of transcendence. The features described below are: acceptance of one's life circumstances, contentment, positive life purpose, industriousness, determination, kindness and compassion, altruism, forgiveness, ethicality, silent repetition and chanting of God's name, maintaining an awareness of God, and doing pilgrimage, kirtan, pravachan, bhajan, japa, dev pooja, aarati, etc. These features are only examples and not an exhaustive list. These few examples are mentioned here and briefly described below to illustrate how simple practices in everyday life can facilitate spiritual development.

Horizontal Dimension of Transcendence

As outlined in Chapter 9, the horizontal and vertical dimensions of transcendence are the dimensions of spirituality. The horizontal dimension of transcendence reflects how one functions in relation to others, such as a sense connection with others, with the community, and possibly with all creatures. The vertical dimension of transcendence reflects how one maintains a connection with the sacred, which may be viewed and labelled in various ways as the higher power, higher self, inner self, higher consciousness, pure consciousness, transcendental reality, the divine or God. Here are some ways that may facilitate progress on the horizontal dimension of transcendence.

Acceptance of one's life circumstances, life obligations and life events may facilitate progress on the horizontal dimension of transcendence. There are several aspects of one's life that are beyond one's control and for which one may not have a justification from a rational perspective. For example, one's physical characteristics, intelligence, the kind of parents one is born to, etc., are decided by factors beyond one's control and yet can have tremendous impact on one's life. The acceptance of such uncontrollable aspects of one's life circumstances can lower negative emotions such as grief, frustration and sadness, lower the possibility of dysfunctional responses such as actions coming out of negative emotions, and allow a constructive focus of one's energy on doing positive work for the self and others. Thus, a sense of acceptance can help avoid negative feelings and actions, and facilitate positive work. This is conducive to spiritual development.

Contentment is another feature. No matter how favourable one's life circumstances are, there is always a possibility that the circumstances of a few other persons will be more favourable. Having contentment can prevent feelings such as envy toward others, and can also prevent actions driven by a desire to possess what others have. As there will always be some persons whose life circumstances are more favourable than one's own, the envy, desire and greed coming from a lack of contentment are likely to have no end. Such envy and greed can be a source of obstruction in the spiritual development process as reflected in various scriptures. In this context, contentment can prevent obstruction in spiritual development.

Positive life purpose is another feature. While some of life's circumstances are beyond one's control, and acceptance and contentment are necessary, it is necessary to engage in constructive actions in order to avoid dysfunctional behaviour such as lethargy, inactivity and laziness, which as per the scriptures are undesirable for spiritual development. A positive life purpose can prevent such negative features by creating a need for constructive actions. Such purpose can be found in day-to-day duties such as serving one's ageing parents, being grateful to one's parents' past contributions to one's life and making reciprocating contributions to them, and by acquiring education in order to be of worthy service to one's community in particular and humanity in general. Also, one can spend one's energies in managing a decent living for oneself so that one can contribute to society, while positively shaping one's own life. Therefore, it is not surprising that the scientific literature on spirituality refers to having a sense of purpose or meaning as one of the features of spirituality. Actions in the pursuit of such a positive purpose are likely to constitute constructive work, virtuous work, or what scriptures refer to as pious work, beneficial for spiritual development.

Industriousness is another feature. Working toward a positive life purpose in an industrious manner can activate and draw on one's emotional, intellectual and physical energies in a positive direction. This way, whatever you see to be your ultimate gifts get fully and positively used in the service of self, humanity, the whole of existence, and thereby and indirectly in the service of nature or God.

Determination is another feature. There are likely to be obstructions when one industriously works toward a positive life purpose. Determination can help in ensuring that one does not cease to work toward one's purpose. It can be described as the exertion of efforts in pursuit of a positive life purpose and sustained occurrence of virtuous actions or pious deeds. Courage can strengthen determination, and persistence comes out of determination. This way, courage, determination and persistence can operate together to facilitate sustained efforts in pursuit of a positive life purpose and for performing virtuous actions.

Kindness and compassion are also to be considered. Suffering, pain and grief are the realities of life. Expressing kindness and compassion towards those who are afflicted with these can alleviate the suffering of others, and help others to focus their energy on positive actions. In this way, the expression of kindness and compassion constitutes virtuous action. Furthermore, while working towards the benefit of others, this constitutes a recognition of one's sense of connection with others. In other words, this indirectly reflects an awareness that all creatures are interconnected in the sense that we all are parts of one whole creation or existence. Such an awareness of a connection with others is mentioned in both the scriptures and in the scientific literature on spirituality. Therefore, it is understandable that the scriptures mention kindness and compassion as divine virtues or qualities of those who are on the path of spiritual development.

Altruism is another feature. Altruism is reflected in performing actions that seek to enhance the welfare of others without seeking material benefits for oneself, which possibly allows one to transcend one's material self. Altruism is an important element of spirituality in the scriptures.

Forgiveness is another feature. In life, there are occasions when one is adversely affected by the deeds of others. This could induce emotions such as grief, sadness, anger and also an urge to take action aimed at taking revenge for the wrongdoing of others. These negative emotions and the resulting negative actions can be curtailed when one experiences forgiveness. As a result, one's energy and capabilities remain available for positive actions that could facilitate progress on the horizontal dimension of transcendence. It is therefore not surprising that forgiveness is regarded as an element of spirituality in the scriptures.

Ethicality is another feature. Truthfulness, honesty, non-violence or avoiding harm to others, etc., are manifestations of ethicality. Avoiding harm to others has a broad connotation, as it may get expressed in several ways, such as not depriving others of what they possess, not seeking undeserved gains, and being fair to others in the sense of not harming their self-interests. In a broader sense, ethicality is grounded in the acknowledgement that all beings are interconnected, that one is a part of the collective or the universe, and thus causing harm to the well-being of others amounts to harming the collective and indirectly oneself. In this sense, upholding ethicality is a way of recognizing a sense of connection with others and with the universe. Thus, ethicality acknowledges the interconnectedness of existence that is included as an aspect of spirituality both in scriptures and in the scientific literature on spirituality.

Vertical Dimension of Transcendence

Existence of the horizontal dimension of transcendence in one's functioning is only one aspect of transcendence or spiritual development. The vertical dimension of transcendence is another aspect of spirituality. The vertical dimension of transcendence is reflected in having a sense of connection with the sacred, which may be viewed and labelled in various ways such as the higher power, higher self, inner self, higher consciousness, pure consciousness, the divine or God. Various features of one's functioning can facilitate such a connection and facilitate progress along the vertical dimension of transcendence. Some of such features are described below.

Different religious traditions have different methods or practices to facilitate a connection with the sacred. For example, the practices or methods that are associated with the Hindu religion for connecting with God include offering prayers, worshipping deities, singing lyrics that praise God, describe the glories of God and seek God's blessings, paying obeisance to God, fasting on certain days regarded as auspicious because of their association with God or fasting as an expression of devotion to God, chanting God's holy names, doing silent repetition of God's holy names, reading scriptures, and doing pilgrimage.

In general, any act or practice that reminds oneself that some sacred or higher power exists and makes one feel that one is remembering, respecting, glorifying, approaching or obeying that conception of the sacred or higher power can facilitate a connection with the sacred, and nourish the vertical dimension of transcendence. For example, lighting a lamp before some deity or even a mental conception of the sacred or God reflects one's acceptance of the existence of the sacred or God and respect or veneration for it, and could serve as a way of connecting with the sacred or God. Thus, several acts or practices that may be available in religions or even personally devised practices that allow one to remember, respect, glorify, approach or obey the sacred or God could serve as a way of having some connection with the sacred or God, and can facilitate the development of the vertical dimension of transcendence.

Meditation is one distinct and broad category of practice for facilitating the vertical dimension of transcendence. There are different forms of meditations and some of these forms are associated with specific religions or scriptures. For example, transcendental meditation is associated with the Vedic literature[1], and the mindfulness approach is associated with Buddhism and involves having an awareness and non-judgemental acceptance of one's ongoing experiences.[2] Most of the significant meditation approaches have as their main element either concentration of attention or mindfulness (mindful or broadened attention), or some combination of these two.[3] Possibly, the practice of meditation facilitates the development of a different form of awareness or consciousness that may be non-material in the sense of being transcendental, and this facilitates the progress along the vertical dimension of transcendence and spiritual development.

Silent repetition and chanting of God's name is another practice. Baai had adopted various means of having a connection with the sacred or God. During the early and middle phase of Baai's life, when she had a strenuous work routine, Baai would chant God's holy name while being engaged in work and she would also do silent repetition of God's holy name while performing her work. In this phase of Baai's life, she did not have the time to separately or exclusively devote to chanting God's name or do silent repetition of God's name, but she still did such chanting or repetition while being engaged in her work.

Maintaining an awareness of God during functioning can also facilitate a connection with God. Baai maintained an awareness that the strenuous work that had come her way was her God-ordained duty, and that she was serving God in others and God itself by doing her work. Baai would also listen to the scriptures and reflect on their contents. This is one way of maintaining awareness of God.

Pilgrimage, kirtan, pravachan, bhajan, japa, dev pooja and aarati are some of the ways of seeking a connection with God and vertical transcendence. Baai would only occasionally go on pilgrimage because her poverty and her multiple work commitments at home did not make it feasible for her to frequently go on pilgrimage. Whenever the circumstances provided Baai access to kirtan and pravachan, Baai most reverentially attended these. As Baai became old, was freed from the strenuous work routine present in the earlier periods of her life, and had time at her disposal, she would engage in individual practices of dev pooja, aarati and japa. In Baai's old age, she also engaged in the group practices of bhajan and group-based paaraayan. Thus, various practices for having a connection with the sacred or God were a part of Baai's life and functioning. Some of such practices changed depending on aspects such as the extent of work demands, her age and time availability.

Interconnection of Horizontal and Vertical Dimensions

It was outlined in Chapter 9 of this book that there is likely to be a relationship between the horizontal dimension of transcendence and the vertical dimension of transcendence, such that progress on one dimension is likely to contribute to progress on the other dimension. Thus, one can simultaneously focus on the features outlined earlier as facilitating progress on the horizontal dimension of transcendence as well as on the vertical dimension of transcendence.

Horizontal transcendence, vertical transcendence, karma yoga and bhakti yoga are labels used in scientific literature and scriptures, and these labels reflect certain ways of functioning in one's life. Possibly, spiritual development is an outcome of how one functions in dealing with one's life circumstances and duties, and maintains an awareness of and a link to some sacred source, force or entity as conceived by oneself based on one's religious or spiritual inclination. Such functioning can facilitate spiritual development that can then be labelled as horizontal and vertical transcendence or karma yoga and bhakti yoga. Thus, spirituality is not separate from life; it is only a way of living one's ordinary life. And this way of living life is feasible for everyone. The description of Baai's life and the spiritual elements in it clearly elucidate the spiritual elements in both the scientific literature and the scriptures. This provides the readers an aspirational avenue to reflect on how they can—in light of their own life circumstances, religion and spiritual inclination—function in order to facilitate their progress on the horizontal and vertical dimensions of transcendence and attain spiritual development.

GLEANINGS

- Life is characterized by uncontrollable but impactful aspects such as one's physical appearance, intelligence, the nature of parents one is born to, etc. Unpredictable events take place with a potential to induce loss and grief.
- Life is full of certainty of the weakening of physical capabilities, emergence of illnesses, gradual and irreversible weakness, and eventual death.
- To contribute, within the limitations of one's circumstances and capabilities, to all of interconnected existence possibly imparts a sense of purpose to life. These aspects possibly reflect the design of nature. Life offers the potential to understand this design, obey it, and thereby experience peace while and through functioning in one's ordinary life.
- Acceptance, contentment, positive life purpose, industriousness, determination, kindness and compassion, forgiveness, ethicality, etc., in one's functioning can help in acknowledging and honouring the design of nature, the sacred, divinity or God, facilitating one's progress on the horizontal dimension of self-transcendence or spiritual development.
- Prayers, obeisance, worship, repetition of God's name or the holy name, reading scriptures, listening to scriptures, etc., are the ways—varying in form across different religious

faith traditions—of seeking a connection with the sacred, divine or God, and facilitating the nurturing of the vertical dimension of self-transcendence or spiritual development.
- The actions that nurture the vertical dimension of transcendence or spiritual development seem to involve acknowledging, affirming belief in, and respecting the design of nature, the sacred, the divine or God, while the actions that nurture the horizontal dimension seem to involve obeying that design in one's functioning in the world.
- The horizontal and vertical dimensions of self-transcendence or spiritual development mutually benefit each other. Both karma and bhakti yoga may be viewed as consisting of actions that nourish both the vertical and horizontal dimensions of self-transcendence or spiritual development by acknowledging that life and creation are a design emanating from a source—nature, the sacred, the divine, God—beyond oneself and obeying that design in one's functioning in life. This way, there is a convergence in the views of functioning conducive to self-transcendence or spiritual development reflected in the scientific literature on spirituality and in the scriptures.
- Both the horizontal and vertical dimensions of self-transcendence or spiritual development, which are included in and facilitate karma yoga and bhakti yoga, can be nurtured through one's functioning while living one's ordinary life.
- To conclude, the earlier parts of this book provide a concrete example of such functioning in the ordinarily lived life by Baai. Chapters 9 and 10 draw upon the scientific literature

on spirituality and upon scriptures, respectively, to trace the spiritual elements in the life lived by her. It is hoped that altogether these chapters will provide guidance in seeking spiritual development through routine functioning while living an ordinary life.

Notes

Introduction

1. The sacred text *Dnyaneshwari*, written by Marathi saint Shri Dnyaneshwar Ji in the thirteenth century in the form of a commentary on Shrimad Bhagavad Gita, mentions that a state of making a passage out of the physical body for someone who has reached the highest form of spiritual development is known as brahma-bhava. This suggests the oneness of the mind with the supreme soul (the Brahman), and at the time of leaving the body, the intellect is not devoured by delusion, the memory is active, and the faculties remain intact.
2. This is reflected in some verses of Shrimad Bhagavad Gita (Chapter 8, Verses 5–10) and some verses of *Dnyaneshwari* (Chapter 8, Verses 60, 68, 69, 74–79, 81–85, 91, 96–99).
3. Based on Verses 60, 68, 69, 74 and 75 from Chapter 8 of *Dnyaneshwari*, which elaborate on Verses 5 and 6 respectively from Chapter 8 of Shrimad Bhagavad Gita
4. Based on Verses 76, 77 and 79 from Chapter 8 of *Dnyaneshwari*, which elaborate on Verse 7 from Chapter 8 of Shrimad Bhagavad Gita
5. Based on Verses 81–85 from Chapter 8 of *Dnyaneshwari*

Chapter 1: A Short Childhood and an Early Marriage

1. Devadikar, B. (ed.), 'Abhanga Number 3115', *Subodh Shri Tukaram Gatha*, Adarsh Vidyarthi Prakashan, Pune, 2008, pp. 667–68.

Chapter 2: The Middle Phase of Baai's Life

1. Verse 48 in Chapter 2 of Shrimad Bhagavad Gita and of Prabhupada's *Bhagavad Gita as It Is*
2. 'Chapter 2, Verse 56', Shrimad Bhagavad Gita, Gita Press, Gorakhpur, 1995.
3. 'Chapter 12, Verse 13', Shrimad Bhagavad Gita, Gita Press, Gorakhpur, 1995.
4. 'Chapter 18, Verse 7', Shrimad Bhagavad Gita, Gita Press, Gorakhpur, 1995.
5. 'Chapter 18, Verse 8', Shrimad Bhagavad Gita, Gita Press, Gorakhpur, 1995.
6. 'Chapter 18, Verse 9', Shrimad Bhagavad Gita, Gita Press, Gorakhpur, 1995.
7. Verse 207 in Chapter 18 of *Dnyaneshwari* elaborating on Verse 9 from Chapter 18 of Shrimad Bhagavad Gita
8. Verse 210 in Chapter 18 of *Dnyaneshwari* elaborating on Verse 9 from Chapter 18 of Shrimad Bhagavad Gita

Chapter 3: The Later Phase of Baai's life

1. Devadikar, B. (ed.), 'Abhanga Number 870', *Subodh Shri Tukaram Gatha*, Adarsh Vidyarthi Prakashan, Pune, 2008.
2. Devadikar, B. (ed.), 'Abhanga Number 3003', *Subodh Shri Tukaram Gatha*, Adarsh Vidyarthi Prakashan, Pune, 2008.
3. 'Chapter 6, Verses 6–7', Shrimad Bhagavad Gita, Gita Press, Gorakhpur, 1995.
4. 'Chapter 17, Verse 19', Shrimad Bhagavad Gita, Gita Press, Gorakhpur, 1995.
5. Bhave, V. (ed.), *Eknathanchi Bhajane*, 10th Edition, Paramdham Prakashan, Wardha, 2011.
6. 'Abhanga Number 18', *Shri Pancharatna Hari-Paath*, Amol Prakashan, Pune, 2014, pp. 13–14.

Chapter 4: The Old-Age Phase of Baai's Life

1. Devadikar, B. (ed.), 'Abhanga Number 762', *Subodh Shri Tukaram Gatha*, Adarsh Vidyarthi Prakashan, Pune, 2008.

2. 'Chapter 5, Verse 25', Shrimad Bhagavad Gita, Gita Press, Gorakhpur, 1995; 'Chapter 12, Verse 4', Shrimad Bhagavad Gita, Gita Press, Gorakhpur, 1995.
3. Piedmont, R.L., 'Does Spirituality Represent the Sixth Factor of Personality? Spiritual Transcendence and the Five-Factor Model', *Journal of Personality*, Vol. 67, No. 6, 1999, pp. 985–1013.

Chapter 5: Baai's Declining Health and Her Journey towards Her Eternal Abode

1. Shrimad Bhagavad Gita (Chapter 8, Verse 23) and the associated elaboration from *Dnyaneshwari* (Chapter 8, Verses 209–10) on this is relevant. An approximate meaning of Verses 209 and 210 from Chapter 8 of *Dnyaneshwari* is that for those who have experienced oneness with the supreme soul (Brahman) at the time of leaving the physical body, their intellect and thinking are not devoured by delusion, their memory is not blinded, their mind is not dead, and all their faculties of consciousness remain fresh and vibrant. Further, Shrimad Bhagavad Gita (Chapter 8, Verse 10) and the associated elaboration from *Dnyaneshwari* (Chapter 8, Verses 91 and 96–99) also provide a relevant description. An approximate meaning of Verses 91 and 96–99 from Chapter 8 of *Dnyaneshwari* is as follows: 'The one who knows and with a steady mind remembers the Brahman at the time of leaving the physical body, he becomes (reaches) the Brahman and leaves his physical body as easily as the sound of a bell gradually diminishes or the lamp flame gradually dims and disappears.'

This is that state that is attained by maintaining a continual connectedness with God all through one's life. This is suggested in Shrimad Bhagavad Gita (Chapter 8, Verse 6) and the associated elaboration from *Dnyaneshwari* (Chapter 8, Verses 74 and 75). The approximate meaning of Verses 74 and 75 from *Dnyaneshwari* is as follows: 'Whatever one has craved for through one's life is what one's mind remembers at the time of leaving one's body. At the time of leaving the physical body, whatever one's mind remembers the same form it takes [in the next birth].'

Therefore, one must ceaselessly remember God through one's life. *Dnyaneshwari* states that this state of union with God or the divine—characterized by being able to leave one's physical body serenely and while the intellect, thinking, memory and mind remain fresh and vibrant—is attained only when God's remembrance is maintained continually throughout one's life.

2. Kalindi (ed.), *Prempanth Ahinsecha: Vinobanchi Jivankatha Tyanchyach Shabdant*, 7th Edition, Paramdham Prakashan, Wardha, 2018, pp. 295–96.

3. 'Chapter 8, Verse 6', Shrimad Bhagavad Gita, Gita Press, Gorakhpur, 1995.

4. 'Chapter 8, Verse 7', Shrimad Bhagavad Gita, Gita Press, Gorakhpur, 1995.

Chapter 6: Baai: An Embodiment of Noble Virtues

1. Tandale, D. (ed.), 'Chapter 18, Verse 160', *Dnyaneshwari*, Amol Prakashan, Pune, 2016.

2. Tandale, D. (ed.), 'Chapter 18, Verse 906', *Dnyaneshwari*, Amol Prakashan, Pune, 2016.

3. Tandale, D. (ed.), 'Chapter 18, Verse 911', *Dnyaneshwari*, Amol Prakashan, Pune, 2016.

4. Tandale, D. (ed.), 'Chapter 10, Verse 118', *Dnyaneshwari*, Amol Prakashan, Pune, 2016.

5. Tandale, D. (ed.), 'Chapter 18, Verse 1359', *Dnyaneshwari*, Amol Prakashan, Pune, 2016.

Chapter 8: Baai's Approach to the Adversities of Life

1. Devadikar, B. (ed.), 'Abhanga Number 1317', *Subodh Shri Tukaram Gatha*, Adarsh Vidyarthi Prakashan, Pune, 2008, p. 285.

2. Devadikar, B. (ed.), 'Abhanga Number 3002', *Subodh Shri Tukaram Gatha*, Adarsh Vidyarthi Prakashan, Pune, 2008, pp. 644–45.

3. Devadikar, B. (ed.), 'Abhanga Number 2294', *Subodh Shri Tukaram Gatha*, Adarsh Vidyarthi Prakashan, Pune, 2008, pp. 496–97.

4. Devadikar, B. (ed.), 'Abhanga Number 2293', *Subodh Shri Tukaram Gatha*, Adarsh Vidyarthi Prakashan, Pune, 2008, p. 496; Devadikar, B. (ed.), 'Abhanga Number 3002', *Subodh Shri Tukaram Gatha*, Adarsh Vidyarthi Prakashan, Pune, 2008, pp. 644–45.
5. 'Chapter 12, Verses 13–19', Shrimad Bhagavad Gita, Gita Press, Gorakhpur, 1995.
6. 'Chapter 13, Verses 7–11', Shrimad Bhagavad Gita, Gita Press, Gorakhpur, 1995.
7. 'Chapter 16, Verses 1–3', Shrimad Bhagavad Gita, Gita Press, Gorakhpur, 1995.
8. 'Chapter 12, Verses 13–19', Shrimad Bhagavad Gita, Gita Press, Gorakhpur, 1995.
9. 'Chapter 16, Verse 5', Shrimad Bhagavad Gita, Gita Press, Gorakhpur, 1995.
10. Paloutzian, R.F., R.A. Emmons and S.G. Keortge, 'Spiritual Well-Being, Spiritual Intelligence, and Healthy Workplace Policy', *Handbook of Workplace Spirituality and Organizational Performance*, R.A. Giacalone and C.L. Jurkiewicz (eds), M.E. Sharpe, Armonk, New York, 2003, p. 87.
11. Fry, L.W., 'Toward a Theory of Ethical and Spiritual Well-Being, and Corporate Social Responsibility through Spiritual Leadership', *Positive Psychology in Business Ethics and Corporate Responsibility*, Information Age Publishing, Greenwich, 2005, p. 56.

Chapter 9: A View Based on the Scientific Literature on Spirituality

1. Piedmont, R.L., et. al., 'The Empirical and Conceptual Value of the Spiritual Transcendence and Religious Involvement Scales for Personality Research', *Psychology of Religion and Spirituality*, Vol. 1, No. 3, 2009, p. 162.
2. Miller, E.D., 'The Development and Validation of a New Measure of Spirituality', *North American Journal of Psychology*, Vol. 6, No. 3, 2004, pp. 423–30.
3. Hill, P.C., and K.I. Pargament, 'Advances in the Conceptualization and Measurement of Religion and Spirituality: Implications for

Physical and Mental Health Research', *American Psychologist*, Vol. 58, No. 1, 2003, p. 65.

4. Seidlitz, L., et. al., 'Development of the Spiritual Transcendence Index', *Journal for the Scientific Study of Religion*, Vol. 41, No. 3, 2002, p. 440.

5. Fry, L.W., 'Toward a Theory of Spiritual Leadership', *The Leadership Quarterly*, Vol. 14, No. 6, 2003, p. 706.

6. Piedmont, R.L., et. al., 'The Empirical and Conceptual Value of the Spiritual Transcendence and Religious Involvement Scales for Personality Research', *Psychology of Religion and Spirituality*, Vol. 1, No. 3, 2009, p. 162.

7. Seidlitz, L., et. al., 'Development of the Spiritual Transcendence Index', *Journal for the Scientific Study of Religion*, Vol. 41, No. 3, 2002, p. 440.

8. Piedmont, R.L., et. al., 'The Empirical and Conceptual Value of the Spiritual Transcendence and Religious Involvement Scales for Personality Research', *Psychology of Religion and Spirituality*, Vol. 1, No. 3, 2009.

9. Hill, P. C., and K.I. Pargament, 'Advances in the Conceptualization and Measurement of Religion and Spirituality: Implications for Physical and Mental Health Research', *American Psychologist*, Vol. 58, No. 1, 2003, pp. 64–65.

10. Ibid.

11. Underwood, L.G., 'The Daily Spiritual Experience Scale: Overview and Results', *Religions*, Vol. 2, 2011, p. 30.

12. Hill, P.C., and K.I. Pargament, 'Advances in the Conceptualization and Measurement of Religion and Spirituality: Implications for Physical and Mental Health Research', *American Psychologist*, Vol. 58, No. 1, 2003, p. 65.

13. Ellison, C.W., 'Spiritual Well-Being: Conceptualization and Measurement', *Journal of Psychology and Theology*, Vol. 11, No. 4, 1983.

14. Benson, P.L., E.C. Roehlkepartain, and S.P. Rude, 'Spiritual Development in Childhood and Adolescence: Toward a Field of Inquiry', *Applied Developmental Science*, Vol. 7, No. 3, 2003.

15. Mirvis, P.H., '"Soul Work" in Organizations', *Organization Science*, Vol. 8, No. 2, 1997, p. 197.
16. Piedmont, R.L., 'Does Spirituality Represent the Sixth Factor of Personality? Spiritual Transcendence and the Five-Factor Model', *Journal of Personality*, Vol. 67, No. 6, 1999, p. 988.
17. Ellison, C.W., 'Spiritual Well-Being: Conceptualization and Measurement', *Journal of Psychology and Theology*, Vol. 11, No. 4, 1983, p. 331.
18. Fry, L.W., 'Toward a Theory of Spiritual Leadership', *The Leadership Quarterly*, Vol. 14, No. 6, 2003, p. 703.
19. Piedmont, R.L., 'Does Spirituality Represent the Sixth Factor of Personality? Spiritual Transcendence and the Five-Factor Model', *Journal of Personality*, Vol. 67, No. 6, 1999.
20. Ellison, C.W., 'Spiritual Well-Being: Conceptualization and Measurement', *Journal of Psychology and Theology*, Vol. 11, No. 4, 1983. p. 383.
21. Benson, P.L., E.C. Roehlkepartain, and S.P. Rude, 'Spiritual Development in Childhood and Adolescence: Toward a Field of Inquiry', *Applied Developmental Science*, Vol. 7, No. 3, 2003, pp. 205–08.
22. Ellison, C.W., 'Spiritual Well-Being: Conceptualization and Measurement', *Journal of Psychology and Theology*, Vol. 11, No. 4, 1983. p. 336.
23. Ibid. 331.
24. Piedmont, R.L., 'Does Spirituality Represent the Sixth Factor of Personality? Spiritual Transcendence and the Five-Factor Model', *Journal of Personality*, Vol. 67, No. 6, 1999.
25. Fry, L.W., 'Toward a Theory of Spiritual Leadership', *The Leadership Quarterly*, Vol. 14, No. 6, 2003, p. 703.
26. Hill, P.C., and K.I. Pargament, 'Advances in the Conceptualization and Measurement of Religion and Spirituality: Implications for Physical and Mental Health Research', *American Psychologist*, Vol. 58, No. 1, 2003, p. 65.
27. Seidlitz, L., et. al., 'Development of the Spiritual Transcendence Index', *Journal for the Scientific Study of Religion*, Vol. 41, No. 3, 2002, p. 440.

28. The term 'transcendent' rather than 'sacred' will be adopted in the subsequent part of this chapter.
29. Ellison, C.W., 'Spiritual Well-Being: Conceptualization and Measurement', *Journal of Psychology and Theology*, Vol. 11, No. 4, 1983.
30. Paloutzian, R.F., R.A. Emmons and S.G. Keortge, 'Spiritual Well-Being, Spiritual Intelligence, and Healthy Workplace Policy', *Handbook of Workplace Spirituality and Organizational Performance*, R.A. Giacalone and C.L. Jurkiewicz (eds), M.E. Sharpe, Armonk, New York, 2003, p. 124.
31. Benson, P.L., E.C. Roehlkepartain, and S.P. Rude, 'Spiritual Development in Childhood and Adolescence: Toward a Field of Inquiry', *Applied Developmental Science*, Vol. 7, No. 3, 2003, p. 208.
32. Piedmont, R.L., 'Does Spirituality Represent the Sixth Factor of Personality? Spiritual Transcendence and the Five-Factor Model', *Journal of Personality*, Vol. 67, No. 6, 1999, p. 988.
33. Ibid.
34. Ibid.
35. Ellison, C.W., 'Spiritual Well-Being: Conceptualization and Measurement', *Journal of Psychology and Theology*, Vol. 11, No. 4, 1983.
36. Moberg, D.O., 'Subjective Measures of Spiritual Well-Being', *Review of Religious Research*, Vol. 25, No. 4, 1984, pp. 351–64.
37. Heaton, D.P., J. Schmidt-Wilk, and F. Travis, 'Constructs, Methods, and Measures for Researching Spirituality in Organizations', *Journal of Organizational Change Management*, Vol. 17, 2004.
38. Seidlitz, L., et. al., 'Development of the Spiritual Transcendence Index', *Journal for the Scientific Study of Religion*, Vol. 41, No. 3, 2002.
39. Newberg, A.B., and D. Monti, 'Neuroscience of Spirituality', *The Palgrave Handbook of Spirituality and Business*, L. Bouckaert and L. Zsolnai (eds), Palgrave Macmillan, Hampshire, 2011, p. 26.
40. Ibid.
41. Hill, P.C., & K.I. Pargament, 'Advances in the Conceptualization and Measurement of Religion and Spirituality: Implications for

Physical and Mental Health Research', *American Psychologist*, Vol. 58, No. 1, 2003; Seidlitz, L., et. al., 'Development of the Spiritual Transcendence Index', *Journal for the Scientific Study of Religion*, Vol. 41, No. 3, 2002.

42. Hill, P.C., and K.I. Pargament, 'Advances in the Conceptualization and Measurement of Religion and Spirituality: Implications for Physical and Mental Health Research', *American Psychologist*, Vol. 58, No. 1, 2003.
43. Kasser, T., 'Materialistic Value Orientation', *The Palgrave Handbook of Spirituality and Business*, L. Bouckaert and L. Zsolnai (eds), Palgrave Macmillan, Hampshire, 2011.
44. Heaton, D.P., J. Schmidt-Wilk, and F. Travis, 'Constructs, Methods, and Measures for Researching Spirituality in Organizations', *Journal of Organizational Change Management*, Vol. 17, 2004.
45. Ibid.
46. Kasser, T., 'Materialistic Value Orientation', *The Palgrave Handbook of Spirituality and Business*, L. Bouckaert and L. Zsolnai (eds), Palgrave Macmillan, Hampshire, 2011.
47. Ibid.
48. Heaton, D.P., J. Schmidt-Wilk, and F. Travis, 'Constructs, Methods, and Measures for Researching Spirituality in Organizations', *Journal of Organizational Change Management*, Vol. 17, 2004.
49. Ibid. 63–64.
50. Fry, L.W., 'Toward a Theory of Spiritual Leadership', *The Leadership Quarterly*, Vol. 14, No. 6, 2003, p. 706.
51. Liu, C.H., and P.J. Robertson, 'Spirituality in the Workplace: Theory and Measurement', *Journal of Management Inquiry*, Vol. 20, No. 1, 2011, pp. 37–38.
52. Bouckaert, L., and L. Zsolnai, 'Spirituality and Business: An Interdisciplinary Overview', *Society and Economy*, Vol. 34, No. 3, 2012, p. 490.
53. Fry, L.W., 'Toward a Theory of Spiritual Leadership', *The Leadership Quarterly*, Vol. 14, No. 6, 2003, p. 705.
54. Ibid.
55. Kolodinsky, R.W., R.A. Giacalone, and C.L. Jurkiewicz, 'Workplace Values and Outcomes: Exploring Personal, Organizational and

Interactive Workplace Spirituality', *Journal of Business Ethics*, Vol. 81, 2008, p. 466.
56. Fry, L.W., 'Toward a Theory of Spiritual Leadership', *The Leadership Quarterly*, Vol. 14, No. 6, 2003, p. 706.
57. Ibid.
58. Bouckaert, L., and L. Zsolnai, 'Spirituality and Business: An Interdisciplinary Overview', *Society and Economy*, Vol. 34, No. 3, 2012, p. 490.
59. Fry, L.W., 'Toward a Theory of Spiritual Leadership', *The Leadership Quarterly*, Vol. 14, No. 6, 2003, p. 703.
60. Ibid.
61. Ibid.

Chapter 10: A View Based on the Scriptures

1. Prabhupada, Bhaktivedanta, *Bhagavad Gita As It Is*, The Bhaktivedanta Book Trust, Mumbai, 2011, p. 2.
2. Ibid.
3. Ibid.
4. Bhave, V. (ed.), *Eknathanchi Bhajane*, Paramdham Prakashan, Wardha, 2011.
5. Verses 182 and 228 from Chapter 2 of *Dnyaneshwari* elaborate on Verses 20 and 28 from Chapter 2 of Shrimad Bhagavad Gita
6. Verses 234 and 237 from Chapter 2 of *Dnyaneshwari* elaborate on Verse 40 from Chapter 2 of Shrimad Bhagavad Gita
7. Verses 264–266 from Chapter 2 of *Dnyaneshwari* elaborate on Verse 47 from Chapter 2 of Shrimad Bhagavad Gita
8. Verses 267–272 from Chapter 2 of *Dnyaneshwari* elaborate on Verse 48 from Chapter 2 of Shrimad Bhagavad Gita
9. Verses 273–274 from Chapter 2 of *Dnyaneshwari* elaborate on Verses 49–50 from Chapter 2 of Shrimad Bhagavad Gita
10. Verses 280–282 of Chapter 2 of *Dnyaneshwari* elaborate on Verse 52 from Chapter 2 of Shrimad Bhagavad Gita
11. Verses 297–300 from Chapter 2 of *Dnyaneshwari* elaborate on Verse 57 from Chapter 2 of Shrimad Bhagavad Gita
12. Verses 301–350 from Chapter 2 of *Dnyaneshwari* elaborate on Verses 58–67 from Chapter 2 of Shrimad Bhagavad Gita

Notes

13. Devadikar, B. (ed.), *Subodh Shri Tukaram Gatha*, Adarsh Vidyarthi Prakashan, Pune, 2008, p. 189.
14. Ibid. 645.
15. Ibid. 782.
16. Shrimad Bhagavad Gita, Gita Press, Gorakhpur, 1995, pp. 57–58.
17. Verses 366 and 367 from Chapter 2 of *Dnyaneshwari* elaborate on Verse 71 from Chapter 2 of Bhagavad Gita.
18. Shrimad Bhagavad Gita, Gita Press, Gorakhpur, 1995, p. 58.
19. Verses 45 and 48 from Chapter 3 of *Dnyaneshwari* elaborate on Verse 4 of Shrimad Bhagavad Gita, and Verse 53 of *Dnyaneshwari* elaborates on Verse 5 from Chapter 3 of Shrimad Bhagavad Gita.
20. Verses 68–71 and 74–76 from Chapter 3 of *Dnyaneshwari* elaborate on Verse 7 from Chapter 3 of Shrimad Bhagavad Gita
21. Shrimad Bhagavad Gita, Gita Press, Gorakhpur, 1995, p. 61.
22. Verses 78 and 80, and 83 and 84 from Chapter 3 of *Dnyaneshwari* elaborate on Verses 8 and 9 respectively from Chapter 3 of Shrimad Bhagavad Gita
23. Verse 97 from Chapter 5 of *Dnyaneshwari* elaborates on Verse 19 from Chapter 5 of Shrimad Bhagavad Gita
24. Verses 115–117, 123 and 124 from Chapter 12 of *Dnyaneshwari* elaborate on Verse 10 from Chapter 12 of Shrimad Bhagavad Gita
25. Verses 43 and 51 from Chapter 6 of *Dnyaneshwari* elaborate on Verse 1, and Verses 52 and 53 from Chapter 6 of *Dnyaneshwari* elaborate on Verse 2 from Chapter 6 of Shrimad Bhagavad Gita
26. Verses 88 and 89 from Chapter 3 of *Dnyaneshwari* elaborate on Verse 10 from Chapter 3 of Shrimad Bhagavad Gita
27. Verses 150 and 151 from Chapter 3 of *Dnyaneshwari* elaborate on Verse 19 from Chapter 3 of Shrimad Bhagavad Gita
28. Verses 169 and 170 from Chapter 3 of *Dnyaneshwari* elaborate on Verse 25 from Chapter 3 of Shrimad Bhagavad Gita
29. Verses 104–110 from Chapter 12 of *Dnyaneshwari* elaborate on Verse 9 from Chapter 12 of Shrimad Bhagavad Gita
30. Such functioning has been referred to in *Dnyaneshwari* Chapters 2–5, 12 and 18.

31. Verses 639–641 and 644 from Chapter 18 of *Dnyaneshwari* elaborate on Verse 26 from Chapter 18 of Shrimad Bhagavad Gita
32. Verses 159 and 160 from Chapter 18 of *Dnyaneshwari* elaborate on Verse 5 from Chapter 18 of Shrimad Bhagavad Gita, and Verse 80 from Chapter 3 of *Dnyaneshwari* elaborates on Verse 8 from Chapter 3 of Shrimad Bhagavad Gita
33. Verses 38 and 39 from Chapter 12 of *Dnyaneshwari* on bhakti yoga elaborate on Verse 2 from Chapter 12 of Shrimad Bhagavad Gita
34. Verse 112 of *Dnyaneshwari* elaborates on Verse 12, and Verses 124 and 126 elaborate on Verses 14 and 15 from Chapter 8 of Shrimad Bhagavad Gita
35. Verses 76–82 from Chapter 12 of *Dnyaneshwari* elaborate on Verse 6 from Chapter 12 of Shrimad Bhagavad Gita
36. Shrimad Bhagavad Gita, Gita Press, Gorakhpur, 1995, p. 190.
37. Verse 126 from Chapter 8 of *Dnyaneshwari* elaborates on Verse 14 from Chapter 8 of Shrimad Bhagavad Gita. Many other verses also suggest this: *Dnyaneshwari* (Verses 97, 98, 101 and 102 from Chapter 12 elaborate on Verse 8 from Chapter 12 of Shrimad Bhagavad Gita) suggests that by engaging with devotion, mind and intellect in God, one attains union with God because with mind and intellect, ego also follows (and gets engaged in or dissolved in God). Elsewhere in *Dnyaneshwari*, a similar view is reflected. *Dnyaneshwari* (Verse 688 from Chapter 11 elaborates on Verse 54 from Chapter 11 of Shrimad Bhagavad Gita) suggests that with all one's devotion directed only at God, one unites with God. *Dnyaneshwari* (Verse 517 from Chapter 9 elaborates on Verse 34 from Chapter 9 of Shrimad Bhagavad Gita) suggests that one should fill one's mind with God, feel loving devotion to God, and pay obeisance to God dwelling in the entire existence. *Dnyaneshwari* (Verse 37 from Chapter 12 elaborates on Verse 2 from Chapter 2 of Shrimad Bhagavad Gita) suggests that one's devotion to God should be like a river that, even after entering an ocean, keeps

immersing in the ocean due to the force of the river's trailing tides. This possibly suggests that one's devotion to God should keep intensifying.

38. Verses 97, 98, 101 and 102 from Chapter 12 of *Dnyaneshwari* elaborate on Verse 8 from Chapter 12 of Shrimad Bhagavad Gita
39. Verses 114–124 from Chapter 12 of *Dnyaneshwari* elaborate on Verse 10 from Chapter 12 of Shrimad Bhagavad Gita
40. Devadikar, B. (ed.), *Subodh Shri Tukaram Gatha*, Adarsh Vidyarthi Prakashan, Pune, 2008, p. 189.
41. Verse 120 from Chapter 12 of *Dnyaneshwari* elaborates on Verse 10 from Chapter 12 of Shrimad Bhagavad Gita
42. Verses 125–131 and 134–140 from Chapter 12 of *Dnyaneshwari* elaborate on Verse 11 from Chapter 12 of Shrimad Bhagavad Gita
43. Verse 205 from Chapter 18 of *Dnyaneshwari* elaborates on Verse 9 from Chapter 18 of Shrimad Bhagavad Gita.
44. Verse 136 from Chapter 12 of *Dnyaneshwari* elaborates on Verse 11 from Chapter 12 of Shrimad Bhagavad Gita. A similar view emerges from *Dnyaneshwari* (Verse 48 from Chapter 3 elaborates on Verse 4 from Chapter 3 of Shrimad Bhagavad Gita), which suggests that to reach the state of an absence of desire-driven work (*naishkarmya-padi*), one has to perform God-ordained duties. A similar view also emerges from *Dnyaneshwari* (Verse 154 from Chapter 18 elaborates on Verse 5 from Chapter 18 of Shrimad Bhagavad Gita), which suggests that after doing considerable God-ordained and mind-purifying work, one reaches the state of an absence of desire-driven work ('naishkarmya' state). These various verses suggest that by doing work for God-ordained duties while relinquishing the work outcomes, such work itself can eliminate the urge for desire-driven and ego-driven work and the (use of) the body itself can be a source of liberation from the sense of self as a physical body.
45. Verse 134 from Chapter 12 of *Dnyaneshwari* elaborates on Verse 11 from Chapter 12 of Shrimad Bhagavad Gita
46. Verse 118 from Chapter 10 of *Dnyaneshwari* elaborates on Verse 8 from Chapter 10 of Shrimad Bhagavad Gita

47. Shrimad Bhagavad Gita, Gita Press, Gorakhpur, 1995, pp. 112-115.
48. These divine virtues (satgunas) are mentioned as a part of the description of bhakti yoga (union with God through devotion) in Chapter 12 of Shrimad Bhagavad Gita and *Dnyaneshwari*. As outlined above, the practice of divine virtues is a way of attaining connection with God through bhakti yoga. Thus, divine virtues mentioned in other chapters of Shrimad Bhagavad Gita and *Dnyaneshwari* could also be considered here. *Dnyaneshwari* (in several verses from Chapter 13 elaborating on Verses 7 to 11 from Chapter 13 of Shrimad Bhagavad Gita) describes the qualities of those who attain the knowledge of God.
49. Verses 184 and Verses 263, 269, 340, 353, 360, 462, 464, 474, 478, 479, 493, 499, 501, 504, 526, 527, 601, 608, 616, and 618 from Chapter 13 of *Dnyaneshwari* elaborate respectively on Verse 6 and Verses 7–11 from Chapter 13 of Shrimad Bhagavad Gita
50. Verses 77, 78, 86–88, 97, 98, 106 and 113 from Chapter 16 of *Dnyaneshwari* elaborate on Verse 1 from Chapter 16 of Shrimad Bhagavad Gita; Verses 114, 124, 154, 155, 159, 161, 166 and 167 from Chapter 16 of *Dnyaneshwari* elaborate on Verse 2 from Chapter 16 of Shrimad Bhagavad Gita; and Verses 199–204 from Chapter 16 of *Dnyaneshwari* elaborate on Verse 3 from Chapter 16 of Shrimad Bhagavad Gita
51. 'Chapter 16, Verse 5', Shrimad Bhagavad Gita, Gita Press, Gorakhpur, 1995.
52. *Dnyaneshwari* (Verses 683–685 from Chapter 11 elaborate on Verse 53 and Verses 686–688 from Chapter 11 elaborate on Verse 54 from Chapter 11 of Shrimad Bhagavad Gita) suggests that the union with God becomes easily feasible when one's mind is filled with intense devotion to God. *Dnyaneshwari* (verses 694 and 695 from Chapter 11 elaborate on Verse 54 from Chapter 11 of Shrimad Bhagavad Gita) suggests that those who see God's visual form lose their ego, and the loss of ego results in union with God.
53. Verses 696–699 of *Dnyaneshwari* elaborate on Verse 55 from Chapter 11 of Shrimad Bhagavad Gita.

54. Verses 91 and 96–99 from Chapter 8 of *Dnyaneshwari* elaborate on Verses 9 and 10 from Chapter 8 of Shrimad Bhagavad Gita.

Chapter 11: Reflections on Practical Spirituality

1. Heaton, D.P., J. Schmidt-Wilk, and F. Travis, 'Constructs, Methods, and Measures for Researching Spirituality in Organizations', *Journal of Organizational Change Management*, Vol. 17, 2004.
2. Shian-Ling Keng, Moria J. Smoski, and Clive J. Robins, 'Effects of Mindfulness on Psychological Health: A Review of Empirical Studies', *Clinical Psychology Review*, Vol. 31, No. 6, 2011.
3. Dunn, B.R., J.A. Hartigan, and W.L. Mikulas, 'Concentration and Mindfulness Meditations: Unique Forms of Consciousness?', *Applied Psychophysiology and Biofeedback*, Vol. 24, 1999.

Acknowledgements

I gratefully acknowledge the support, facilitation and benevolence of several institutes and individuals. My first and foremost expression of gratitude is toward my late father and my late mother who, through their nobly lived lives, deeds and words, have profoundly impacted my life, ideals and work. There are several individuals—they cannot be identified by name—who suffered because of me. I am grateful to them for their sacrifice, tolerance and forgiveness. I gratefully acknowledge my indebtedness to them with my prayers for forgiveness. I am grateful to the various institutes that provided me help, education and work, for their contribution to the evolution of my life. There are several individuals who supported and helped me during my education and academic career. With gratitude, I acknowledge, without naming them individually, their kindness, understanding and support. I am also grateful to Dr Payal Kumar, who helped in identifying a suitable publisher for the book and also helped by editing the book text. I am grateful to the entire team of Rupa Publications for helping me through the editorial processes of making this book, which is my mother's posthumous service to humanity, available for its potential beneficiaries.

The contents of this book reflect my recollection and reconstruction of what I had observed, sensed and heard about the life described in this book, and my interpretation of it and of the literature. I pray for forgiveness from all if there is any error in the contents. My mother's life was a life of service and devotion. I pray that her life's limited depiction reflected in this book also renders a benign service to the world.

References

Benson, P.L., E.C. Roehlkepartain, and S.P. Rude, 'Spiritual Development in Childhood and Adolescence: Toward a Field of Inquiry', *Applied Developmental Science*, Vol. 7, No. 3, 2003.

Bhave, V. (ed.), *Eknathanchi Bhajane*, Paramdham Prakashan, Wardha, 2011.

Chandler, C.K., J.M. Holden, and C.A. Kolander, 'Counseling for Spiritual Wellness: Theory and Practice', *Journal of Counseling & Development*, Vol. 71, 1992.

Devadikar, B. (ed.), *Subodh Shri Tukaram Gatha*, Adarsh Vidyarthi Prakashan, Pune, 2008.

Ellison, C.W., 'Spiritual Well-Being: Conceptualization and Measurement', *Journal of Psychology and Theology*, Vol. 11, No. 4, 1983.

Fry, L.W., 'Toward a Theory of Ethical and Spiritual Well-Being, and Corporate Social Responsibility through Spiritual Leadership', *Positive Psychology in Business Ethics and Corporate Responsibility*, Information Age Publishing, Greenwich, 2005.

Fry, L.W., 'Toward a Theory of Spiritual Leadership', *The Leadership Quarterly*, Vol. 14, No. 6, 2003.

Giacalone, R.A., and C.L. Jurkiewicz, 'Right from Wrong: The Influence of Spirituality on Perceptions of Unethical Business Activities', *Journal of Business Ethics*, Vol. 46, 2003.

Heaton, D.P., J. Schmidt-Wilk, and F. Travis, 'Constructs, Methods, and Measures for Researching Spirituality in Organizations', *Journal of Organizational Change Management*, Vol. 17, 2004.

Hill, P.C., and K.I. Pargament, 'Advances in the Conceptualization and Measurement of Religion and Spirituality: Implications for Physical and Mental Health Research', *American Psychologist*, Vol. 58, No. 1, 2003.

Kalindi (ed.), *Prempanth Ahinsecha: Vinobanchi Jivankatha Tyanchyach Shabdant*, Paramdham Prakashan, Wardha, 2018.

Kasser, T., 'Materialistic Value Orientation', *The Palgrave Handbook of Spirituality and Business*, L. Bouckaert and L. Zsolnai (eds), Palgrave Macmillan, Hampshire, 2011.

Kolodinsky, R.W., R.A. Giacalone, and C.L. Jurkiewicz, 'Workplace Values and Outcomes: Exploring Personal, Organizational and Interactive Workplace Spirituality', *Journal of Business Ethics*, Vol. 81, 2008, p. 466.

Liu, C.H., and P.J. Robertson, 'Spirituality in the Workplace: Theory and Measurement', *Journal of Management Inquiry*, Vol. 20, No. 1, 2011.

Miller, E.D., 'The Development and Validation of a New Measure of Spirituality', *North American Journal of Psychology*, Vol. 6, No. 3, 2004.

Mirvis, P.H., '"Soul Work" in Organizations', *Organization Science*, Vol. 8, No. 2, 1997.

Moberg, D.O., 'Subjective Measures of Spiritual Well-Being', *Review of Religious Research*, Vol. 25, No. 4, 1984.

Newberg, A.B., and D. Monti, 'Neuroscience of Spirituality', *The Palgrave Handbook of Spirituality and Business*, L. Bouckaert and L. Zsolnai (eds), Palgrave Macmillan, Hampshire, 2011.

Newberg, A.B., and D. Monti, 'Neuroscience of Spirituality', *The Palgrave Handbook of Spirituality and Business*, L. Bouckaert and L. Zsolnai (eds), Palgrave Macmillan, Hampshire, 2011.

Paloutzian, R.F., R.A. Emmons, and S.G. Keortge, 'Spiritual Well-Being, Spiritual Intelligence, and Healthy Workplace Policy', *Handbook of Workplace Spirituality and Organizational Performance*, R.A. Giacalone and C.L. Jurkiewicz (eds), M.E. Sharpe, Armonk, New York, 2003.

Piedmont, R.L., 'Does Spirituality Represent the Sixth Factor of Personality? Spiritual Transcendence and the Five-Factor Model', *Journal of Personality*, Vol. 67, No. 6, 1999.

Piedmont, R.L., et. al., 'The Empirical and Conceptual Value of the Spiritual Transcendence and Religious Involvement Scales for Personality Research', *Psychology of Religion and Spirituality*, Vol. 1, No. 3, 2009.

Prabhupada, Bhaktivedanta, *Bhagavad Gita as It Is*, The Bhaktivedanta Book Trust, Mumbai, 2011.

Seidlitz, L., et. al., 'Development of the Spiritual Transcendence Index', *Journal for the Scientific Study of Religion*, Vol. 41, No. 3, 2002.

Shri Pancharatna Hari-Paath, Amol Prakashan, Pune, 2014.

Shrimad Bhagavad Gita, Gita Press, Gorakhpur, 1995.

Tandale, D. (ed.), *Dnyaneshwari*, Amol Prakashan, Pune, 2016.

Underwood, L.G., 'The Daily Spiritual Experience Scale: Overview and Results', *Religions*, Vol. 2, 2011.